DATE DUE

OCT 22			
FEB 17			
MAR 1 0			
MAY 8 '84			
MAY 24 1991			
OCT 31			
MAR 26 1996			
OC 16 '06			
OC 21 '06			
GAYLORD			PRINTED IN U.S.A.

<<<<<<<<<<<<<<<<<<<<<<<<<<<<<<<<<<<<<<<<<<<<<<<<<<<<<<<<<<<<<<<<<<<<

THE STORY OF THE
REVOLUTIONARY WAR

<<<<<<<<<<<<<<<<<<<<<<<<<<<<<<<<<<<<<<<<<<<<<<<<<<<<<<<<<<<<<<<<<<<<

Books by COLONEL RED REEDER

The West Point Stories

WEST POINT PLEBE

WEST POINT YEARLING

WEST POINT SECOND CLASSMAN

WEST POINT FIRST CLASSMAN

In preparation

2ND LT. CLINT LANE: WEST POINT TO BERLIN

THE STORY OF THE CIVIL WAR

THE STORY OF THE REVOLUTIONARY WAR

ATTACK AT FORT LOOKOUT

THE MACKENZIE RAID

THE SHERIFF OF HAT CREEK

WHISPERING WIND

With NARDI REEDER CAMPION

THE WEST POINT STORY

THE STORY OF THE REVOLUTIONARY WAR

by
COLONEL RED REEDER

Illustrations and Maps by
FREDERICK CHAPMAN

DUELL, SLOAN AND PEARCE
New York

For

JULIA POTTER REEDER

CONTENTS

1. "The Fate of a Nation Was Riding That Night"   3

2. Storm Signals   9

3. Tea and Salt Water   15

4. Ethan Allen, Benedict Arnold, and Fort Ticonderoga   25

5. The Battle of Bunker Hill   36

6. General George Washington   44

7. The Attack on Canada   56

8. The Declaration of Independence   65

9. Sergeant Jasper Displays the Spirit of South Carolina   69

10. Desperate Days in New York and New Jersey   76

11. The Spirit of 1776   91

12. Start of the Year of "The Bloody 7's"   99

13. Burgoyne and St. Leger Smash Toward Albany   107

14. Two Battles at Saratoga   114

15. General Howe Captures Philadelphia   124

16. Valley Forge and Results of Saratoga   131

17. Battle of Monmouth   140

18. Privateers—and a French Fleet   145

19. The Battle of Stony Point   153

20. Benedict Arnold   161

21. The Indian Frontier   170

22. Redcoats in the South   182

23. Misery and Mutiny   193

24. The Strange Battle at Kings Mountain—Fight at
    Cowpens   199

25. A Nine-Hundred-Mile March to Victory   207

26. Prisoners of War   214

27. The American Navy   219

28. The Surrender   230

    Author's Note   240

    For Further Reading   241

    Index   245

THE STORY OF THE REVOLUTIONARY WAR

Chapter 1

"THE FATE OF A NATION WAS RIDING THAT NIGHT"

THERE was wild excitement near Boston, Massachusetts. Two lanterns hung in the steeple of the North Church as a signal that the Redcoats were leaving Boston by water. It was midnight. Two dispatch riders, William Dawes and Paul Revere, galloped through the countryside to warn American patriots that the British soldiers would take the road to Concord.

The British leader, Lieutenant General the Honorable Thomas Gage, believed the movement of his Redcoats across the harbor would be a secret. He hoped his men would be well on their way to Concord before the patriots knew what was up. Gage's men were to capture military stores in Concord belonging to the patriots and to bring in two of their leaders, Sam Adams and John Hancock, said to be in that village.

But an American in Boston was watchful. His name was Doctor Joseph Warren. It was Warren who sent the dispatch riders galloping with the stirring news that the British were marching on Concord.

Not only were the American mounted messengers at work, but British officers riding patrol along the principal roads unintentionally alarmed the people. The entire countryside was alert.

3

It was the nineteenth of April, 1775, one of the most fateful days in the history of the world.

The Minutemen had been called out. These were the pick of the colonial militia, men from sixteen to sixty, who agreed to turn out at a minute's notice when there was danger. They were originally organized as protection against the Indians. The Min-

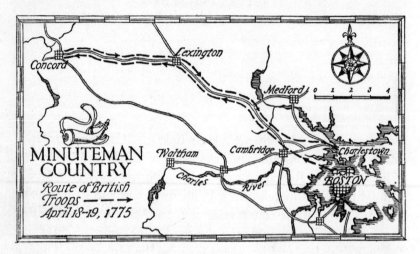

MAP NO. 1

utemen had no uniforms; they drilled in civilian clothes and were expected to fight in them. They elected their officers, which often proved a handicap because the best leaders were not always chosen.

The Minutemen could not drill as well as General Gage's Redcoats, and the Minutemen did not all have the same weapons. Some carried the "Brown Bess" smoothbore muskets, which fired an amazingly heavy bullet (eleven to the pound). A few had "fowling pieces." Other Minutemen carried blunderbusses. Over their shoulders were slung bullet pouches and powder horns. A few owned bayonets. The officers carried flintlock pistols and wore swords; some had spontoons, long spears symbolic of rank, or a short musket. Because colonial troops were not equipped alike, the supply problem was difficult.

There were not many roads in America. It would be hard for the generals to communicate with one another and to maneuver large bodies of troops.[1] And the lack of roads would hinder the British generals as well as the Americans.

The British Army had other troubles, too. It had just been through the Seven Years' War and its regiments had few men. British officers bought their original commissions and promotions. The King of England, George III, wanted to control the patriots, but he did not realize all the problems of placing an army across three thousand miles of rough Atlantic, of housing the army and supplying it.

But, on the other hand, the King had a system for paying his soldiers, traditions that bound the regiments together, and wonderful noncommissioned officers. The Redcoats also shouldered the Brown Bess, and each infantryman carried a twenty-one-inch bayonet. One "weapon" not listed was the iron discipline of the British Regulars—and the Redcoats were just as courageous as the Americans.

The British General Gage was unhappy about sending his troops out of Boston on the mission to Concord. He realized law in America could not be enforced by merely sending troops to the scene. He believed American patriots would fight bravely—but few Englishmen agreed with Gage. King George was determined to bring the colonies to their knees, and the start of his idea was the march on Concord, Massachusetts. For twelve years the Massachusetts Colony had been a thorn in the side of the British government.

The King and his advisers were bringing on the worst type of war—civil war. It would pit friend against friend, family

[1] The lack of roads explains why, in this war, there were so many small fights.

against family, untrained colonists against professional troops from Europe. It would be a war in which one of the greatest characteristics of the English peoples in time of peril, *stubbornness*, would be a trait shared by both sides.

That nineteenth of April was a tragic day for Americans who believed that the colonies should remain forever under the Crown. Such people believed that differences with the mother country should be settled by agreement, that force was unthinkable. It was a glorious day in the minds of patriot leaders who labored to advance the idea that the colonies should be free from England. Sam Adams, the patriot, had written that the most dreaded thing in the world for any man was *slavery*. Many in Massachusetts and in other colonies agreed with Adams.

And Sam Adams was supposed to be in Concord. The senior British officer in the red-clad column marching on that village, Lieutenant Colonel Francis Smith, knew how happy his general would be if he captured the firebrand, Sam Adams.

The sun warmed the marchers. The column of about seven hundred grenadiers and light infantry looked magnificent. The grenadiers wore bearskin hats, which made ordinary men look eight feet tall. The British Regulars swung along—there was nothing in sight to stop them.

But on the triangular-shaped village green at Lexington Captain Jonas Parker inspected seventy Minutemen who had reported for duty. The Minutemen waited. The captain steadied them for the test.

On came the "lobsters," as the patriots called the soldiers of the King. When the advance guard approached, Captain Parker gave the order to his Minutemen, *"Stand your ground! Don't fire unless fired upon! But if they want war, let it begin here!"*

The British Major Pitcairn, commanding the light infantry, and two officers galloped up near the Minutemen. Behind the three officers of the King stretched the Redcoat column. One

of the three officers cried, "Ye villains, ye rebels, disperse! Damn you, disperse!"

The sight of so many British soldiers was too much for the seventy Minutemen, who began to scatter. Someone fired a shot. One of the British officers yelled at his troops, "Fire! By God, fire!"

Maybe the Americans fired first; it has never been accurately determined. A volley crashed into the patriots. Eight men fell dead on the village green—among them Captain Parker. Ten other Minutemen were wounded. Had the Redcoats known, they could have easily captured Sam Adams and John Hancock, who were about two miles away.

The British column re-formed and marched on, weapons glittering in the morning sun. It was hotter, and they had six miles to Concord. The drummers tapped out time so the men could march better. On all sides the English could hear other drums summoning the patriots.

There was great excitement in the little village of Concord when the news from Lexington arrived. Patriots from neighboring towns were arriving. Women gathered children and hustled them to places where they would be safe from the bullets of the Brown Bess muskets.

The British marched into Concord. Some began to search for the stores of military supplies. Two cannons (twenty-four pounders) were found, a few barrels of powder, and some musket balls. That was all. The British worked feverishly to destroy the war supplies and they did not do a good job. Other Redcoats marched out of town to the bridge over the sleepy Concord River, where the patriots had taken a stand. After a short fight at the bridge, the Redcoats began to withdraw toward Boston.

The whole countryside seemed to rise up against them. The patriots poured fire into the British column from the rear and from the sides. The British had sixteen miles to go, back over the crooked roads, to safety, and they were tired from the long march out. The Massachusetts men fired from behind stone walls, trees, and with little semblance of military order or design. At places the fighting was hand-to-hand. There was confusion in the British ranks. The retreat eventually became a rout. By the end of the day the British had lost almost three hundred killed, wounded, or missing; the patriots, ninety-five.

Now, express riders were galloping. The news that fighting had begun on the nineteenth of April in '75 was carried to the other colonies as fast as horse and rider could travel.

Chapter 2

STORM SIGNALS

F<small>AR</small> from Massachusetts—in London—a heavy-set man walking along Craven Street attracted attention. He was dressed handsomely in a round fur hat, white stock at his throat, a generous coat over a fancy vest, breeches, white stockings, and gold buckles on his shoes. Many knew the famous American, Benjamin Franklin.

Ben Franklin at fifty-eight was one of the most amazing people of his time. He was the son of a humble tallow merchant and soapmaker. He was largely self-educated. His first job, in a printing house, enabled him to borrow books. He divided his time at night between reading and teaching himself how to write; he was determined to succeed. Ben Franklin became a printer, bookseller, author, linguist, philosopher noted for his common sense and honesty, and one of our first diplomats. Almost everyone knew how Ben Franklin had flown a kite to obtain electricity from a thunder cloud. He had written and published *Poor Richard's Almanac*, and his wit and pithy observations helped many people.

During the French and Indian War twenty years before Lexington and Concord, Franklin offered money to help the

British general, Braddock, secure wagons to move against the French and Indians at Fort Duquesne.[1] Ben Franklin warned the general that the Indians favored the ambush. But the general paid little attention.

"Braddock's Defeat" was a horrible incident in the French and Indian War. General Braddock and his Regulars were not familiar with Indian-style fighting, and many of his American soldiers were worthless.

[1] The present site of Pittsburgh.

The Indians and French, in fewer numbers, caught this stuffy British general and his command on the Monongahela River. Nine hundred seventy-seven of Braddock's men were killed or wounded in the ambush, and Braddock himself was killed. Numbers of American soldiers ran. Ben Franklin was greatly disappointed in the result.

Franklin, like most Americans, respected King George III. Franklin was agent in London for three colonies: Georgia, New Jersey, and Massachusetts. His job was to help these colonies. He often used his wit in America's behalf. For instance, to belittle the popular idea that America was a place of unlimited wealth, he wrote in the *London Chronicle*, "... the very tails of American sheep are so laden with wool that each sheep has a little car or wagon to support its tail and to keep it from trailing on the ground." Ben also wrote that fisheries on America's Canadian border exhibited one of the finest spectacles in nature, when whales pursuing codfish leaped up the great falls at Niagara. But the English did not see the humor or the thought behind Franklin's words.

Although he was humorous, Ben Franklin saw trouble ahead.

The arguments about governing the colonies in America had been running for years. Each month there had been less understanding between the motherland and her colonies. If, in 1765, you had asked a young Englishman about the American colonies, he might have replied like this:

"We have just won a world war, which they call the Seven Years' War. Part of our reason for fighting was to get the French out of America. We are now the world's greatest colonial power. Each of our American colonies is protected by our navy and army. Our Union Jack flies on every ocean.

"It was just three years ago that the chief of the Ottawa tribe in America, Pontiac, led a bloody uprising. The borders of

Pennsylvania, Maryland, and Virginia went up in flames. Good British soldiers died to protect the Americans. The Indians murdered, burned people at the stake, and captured nine frontier forts. Yes, the Americans fought a little, but nothing compared with our wonderful Redcoats. Had it not been for our soldiers and our leaders, the colonists would have been pushed into the Atlantic, for each colony was interested only in saving its own skin. They did not help one another. So we keep troops in America to protect the colonists from the Indians. It's a bad situation. If we don't protect the colonists we get blamed.

"To keep troops in America costs money. In the colonies are vast lands rich in raw materials. The Seven Years' War increased our national debt tremendously. On top of that, there's the expense of keeping our troops in America. *Who should pay for this?* The British public is already taxed more than it can bear. His Majesty is determined that the colonies share this expense.

"But what do we get for our pains and pounds? I tell you we have a set of ungrateful wretches in America who sit up nights thinking of ways to evade laws. Hotheads. Sam Adams, Patrick Henry, Josiah Quincy, and Alex MacDougall are doing their best to cause trouble.

"Smugglers work on the American coast at night to avoid paying import taxes. They are defrauding the hand that's protecting them. The situation is tragic. We ask the colonies to quarter troops—that is, to house soldiers sent to protect them—and this causes a howl. Howling is the only thing the Americans are united in.

"This great man the Americans sent over here as an agent, Ben Franklin. We're not so sure about him. He says we British have a right to regulate colonial trade but not to lay taxes. What does he mean? He is talking out of both sides of his mouth—something not covered in his *Almanac*.

"King George has a terrible weapon which he may use if things get bad enough: the British Army."

But if you had asked a young patriot living in one of the thirteen colonies about his feelings toward England, he might have replied like this:

"The colonies have been in existence over a hundred and fifty years. Our explorers scouted the wilderness. Our people carved a country out of wild and dangerous territory. This work is still going on. We paid for this country by hard work. It's absurd to think that a parliament three thousand miles across the Atlantic can make laws for us. All they know is what they read in reports and what travelers tell them.

"This is what we are saddled with: A few years ago, King George issued an order closing the region between the Alleghenies and the Mississippi—from Florida to Quebec. We've got almost three million people in America now. Our population is growing. Are we to sit idle and just let the deer and the Indian use these lands till the King is ready to let us settle them?

"Here in América we are divided into three parts. Maybe more. First, there're the patriots—the Whigs. We are the ones who want a change. We are the 'up-setters.' Next, there are the Loyalists, or Tories. They love the King. The Tories believe that the King and his men can do no wrong. And about a third of our people do not care what happens. Hate to tell you this, but it is true. And we're divided even more, for some of our patriots can't be counted upon to shoulder a musket if there is a war. Everyone knows that many English officials are corrupt.

"But it's not just that, nor the weight of the taxes, we object to. We can pay our taxes. It's the *right to tax us* we protest against.

"The quicker Parliament recognizes our problems, the less chance of a split between us and England.

"The law saying we must house British troops is absolutely disgraceful. Would you like to have a company of foreign soldiers in your town? People who overrun your property and at the same time sneer at you? We want no rude Redcoats living in our inns, putting up tents on our commons. Your people think Americans can't fight. *But don't underestimate what Americans can do.*"

Chapter 3

TEA AND SALT WATER

THE English king, George III, had been told over and over by his mother, "George, be King." The great English leader, Sir Winston Churchill, said years later, "George did his best to obey." But when George approved the Stamp Act in 1765, he brought war closer. He was not a great king, for he failed in most of the big problems he faced.

The Stamp Act made Americans pay for tax stamps on legal documents and newspapers. The fee was not heavy but taxing newspapers stirred up the writers, and they stirred up the people. The colonists began to ask, "What are our rights?"

In England, the wise Ben Franklin found himself walking a tight rope. The colonies wanted to have the Stamp Act repealed. Franklin had to work for this, yet he felt he could not afford to irritate the King and his minister, George Grenville, for that would accomplish nothing.

In America, one of the greatest orators of all time addressed the Virginia House of Burgesses. This tall man of twenty-nine had a confident air. His name was Patrick Henry. He had a voice that rang clear, and a trait of coupling words to his voice in a manner that could, when he chose, electrify people. In a speech,

A MAP of the
AMERICAN COLONIES
Showing the Principal Cities
and Battle Grounds. 1775-81

MAP No. 2

Patrick Henry ridiculed the Stamp Act and attacked King George. Henry was interrupted by shouts from the members, *"Treason! Treason!"*

But Henry was not upset. He kept his temper. He answered loudly, *"If this be treason, make the most of it!"* There was great excitement at the meeting. Afterward, a squire from Mount Vernon, Virginia, George Washington, congratulated the young lawyer. "Mister Henry," Washington said, "you have put Virginia at the head of all the colonies."

Up in Massachusetts, a thirty-year-old man of medium stature, with steel-gray eyes and a long nose, reacted vigorously when a ship brought news of the Stamp Act into Boston Harbor. This man, Sam Adams, graduated fifth in his class from Harvard, but he had little trouble doing that, because pupils were ranked by social position. He had made a poor start in life, failing as a brewer, and as a tax collector he had taken public funds.

But now Sam Adams became a man of great importance. In the meeting houses, the taverns, wherever men met, Sam Adams spoke and people listened. He organized the masses in Boston against England. He took his quill pen and wrote a document that startled every one of the eighteen thousand people in the town. In it was the thought. *"If our Trade be taxed, why not our Lands, our Produce ... in short, everything we possess? They tax us without our having legal representation."*

Sam Adams seized every opportunity to attack the King. He worked hard to train other revolutionary leaders. He became the principal leader against the Crown.

With Sam Adams stirring up the workers, discontent grew. A Boston mob sacked the house of Lieutenant Governor Thomas Hutchinson, ruined his wonderful library, and damaged his home. The mob carried off silver plate and furniture. They cared little that Hutchinson had spoken against the Stamp Act and other forms of taxation. Sam Adams had not led the mob, but the printers, sail-makers, dock workers, laborers, and others took his words literally. They believed they were as fit to govern as the King and his Parliament. To the mob, violence seemed the answer.

Sam Adams made his headquarters at the Green Dragon Tavern on Boston's Union Street, and people came for miles to hear him attack the Stamp Act. Because Adams was anxious to keep alive the spirit aroused by the act, he and one of his leaders, John Hancock, organized "The Sons of Liberty."

The Sons of Liberty were at first a wild mob, spurred on by Sam Adams. The howls of conch shells were signals for their meetings. Sam directed the fierce enthusiasm of the Sons against the Tories and Stamp Act officials. Soon the society spread to other colonies. In South Carolina, a mob of five hundred Sons besieged British troops.

A smart and wealthy merchant in South Carolina, who had been educated in England, advanced a new idea. His name was Christopher Gadsden, and he urged the colonies to unite. But Gadsden was ahead of his time. The colonies were not ready. They were jealous of one another. Each colony was afraid it would be forced to bear more than its share of the defense in case of attack by Indians or other enemies.

But, at the suggestion of men in Massachusetts, the colonies held a congress in New York City to discuss the hated Stamp Act. Many great Americans attended. The speeches of Sam Adams, Christopher Gadsden, Patrick Henry, John Dickinson, John Lamb, Dr. Joseph Warren, and Paul Revere were printed in the public press and were widely read. The delegates drew up a polite Declaration of Rights. It said that the colonies should do their own taxing because they were not represented in Parliament. The King was not interested in the Declaration of Rights.

But the colonies suddenly received help from an unexpected

source: the British merchants. These merchants were losing money because organizations like the Sons of Liberty were encouraging people to boycott British goods. "The Great Commoner," as he was called, William Pitt, in one of his speeches, said England had been wrong in her treatment of the colonies, that the Stamp Act should be repealed.

When Parliament repealed the hated Stamp Act, after it had been in force a year, people on both sides of the Atlantic rejoiced. But Ben Franklin and a few others knew the trouble was not over just because the Stamp Act had been canceled. America had become a powder keg. All that was needed for an explosion was someone to light the fuse.

The colonies now lost a friend. William Pitt, who had long championed the cause of the colonies, became sick, and Charles Townshend rose to power in England. Soon, duties were placed on articles shipped in from England: lead, glass, paper, paint, and wine, and the trouble started all over again.

A young man in Boston had, in 1768, inherited from his rich uncle the most prominent merchant business in the city. Many American merchants were smugglers, but none engaged in this illegal business on the scale in which young John Hancock did. Hancock was slightly below medium height and had a nose like a miniature ski slide. He had a fine background. He was a Harvard graduate, but people doubted he could handle his uncle's business. Through St. Andrew's Masonic Lodge, John Hancock met the leading patriots of the city: the plump, eagle-eyed politician, James Otis; the brilliant young writer, Josiah Quincy, who longed for fighting to start; the fiery Sam Adams; and his second cousin, John Adams.

One of John Hancock's vessels, *The Liberty*, arrived in Boston Harbor with wines from Madeira. Out sailed the British custom official to collect the tax due the King. Sailors of *The Liberty* locked the custom agent below decks and hustled the wine ashore. The custom agent was furious. When he was released, he went as fast as he could to the captain of H.M.S. *Romney* (fifty guns), which was in the harbor unloading British troops. The captain of *Romney* saw his duty. In his eyes, *The Liberty* was a smuggler's vessel, so he seized her for evading the laws of entry.

Excitement in Boston reached a new pitch. The Sons called a meeting in Faneuil Hall. John Hancock became a martyr in the eyes of the people.

When news of *The Liberty* reached England, Ben Franklin wrote in the London papers that smuggling was not confined to America, that it had long been a blight on the English coast. He said that most Americans were loyal to the King; that Scotland had had its revolts, and England its plots. He pointed out that the new system of politics tended to separate the two countries.

But the British leaders were in no mood to listen to Ben Franklin. They decided to make Boston feel the might of the empire; so they placed two regiments of Redcoats on eight men-of-war and ordered them to sail for America. When the people of the town saw the Redcoats come ashore, war seemed closer.

For a while it was quiet, for all taxes were lifted except the tax on tea. But calm days did not suit Sam Adams. He was worried for fear the quarrel between the two countries would pass. He and his hot-tempered lieutenants, Otis and Joseph Warren, worked to stir up more trouble.

In 1770, an incident happened that suited Sam Adams and his friends and inflamed the colonies. Young boys in Boston snowballed a British sentry outside the customhouse and the sentry knocked one down. At night a mob gathered. The cry went up, "Fire! Fire!" People poured into the streets. A boy pointed at the

sentry on duty and cried, "That's the scoundrel who knocked me down." Instantly the crowd yelled, *"Let's knock him down! Kill him! Kill him!"*

The British Officer of the Day sent eight Redcoats to the relief of the sentinel. A Negro named Crispus Attucks shouted at the soldiers, "I dare you to fire!" But the soldiers did not. Attucks, and sailors with him, beat the muskets of the soldiers with clubs. A Redcoat fired. Down went Attucks. Other soldiers fired. Three men in the mob were killed, five seriously wounded. News of the "Boston Massacre," as the affair became known, was exaggerated by the time it reached other colonies. This was the spark that lit the powder keg.

Sam Adams now turned all the venom he could muster on the unpopular British soldiers in Boston, in order to have them removed from the town.

Some boys in Boston demonstrated they were not cowed by the British. Redcoats had thrown sand on the hill on which the boys were coasting. The boys went to General Gage's headquarters and asked to see the general. Staff officers laughed and said the general was too busy to see them just because their coast had been ruined. But the boys would not leave until they had seen General Gage himself. In reality, the boys were like their fathers: unafraid.

Trouble continued. The revenue cutter, H.M.S. *Gaspee*, on patrol to stop smuggling off the Rhode Island coast, went aground. A rabble burned her to the water's edge.

"Committees of Correspondence" were set up with the idea of uniting towns and colonies. Sam Adams's tremendous drive helped establish them. The demagogues in America were becoming more and more powerful and, in England, the King worried for fear his government was too easy on the colonists.

Now Lord North, the King's minister, made a bad mistake. The date was 1773. Lord North permitted ships of the East India Tea Company to sell tea in America without paying duty.

When the first ship of the East India Company carrying tea arrived in Boston and tied up at Griffin's Wharf, there was excitement and confusion. Young Josiah Quincy harangued an excited meeting. That night, when two more of the East India Company ships tied up at the wharf, one hundred and twenty persons disguised as Mohawk Indians boarded the ships and cast three hundred and forty-two chests of tea into the harbor.

About seventy-five thousand dollars' worth of tea had been destroyed. When news of the "tea party" reached London, the colonies lost many friends. Many people in Boston thought that the East India Company should receive pay for the tea. The King's ministry struck hard. The port of Boston was closed to overseas trade.

This was a serious thing to the people of the town. The very life of the community was threatened. Boston sent word to the colonies for help, and help came rapidly. Massachusetts gave fish and oil. Connecticut sent hundreds and hundreds of sheep, one flock being driven by Israel Putnam, a hero of the French and Indian War. South Carolina sent rice; Pennsylvania, bread and flour. Virginia sent not only money but barrels of flour numbering almost ten thousand. New York sent meal and brandy; from New Hampshire came cattle and sheep; from Rhode Island, clothing. Money came from Georgia and from friends in England.

Ben Franklin applauded the spirit of the colonies in private letters home, but his position in England was becoming more and more difficult. He could see King George's policies were shortsighted, that England and her colonies were drifting toward war —although the King did not want war. However, the King would not listen to persons who disagreed with him.

In America, the danger of war made the people feel closer together. In September, 1774, the First Continental Congress met in Philadelphia. It was the most important meeting held in America up to that time. Many of the great men of the colonies were there. A message was sent to King George, another to the people of England, and a list of grievances was drawn up. But the King and Parliament were not anxious to listen to a congress —to one colony perhaps, but not to colonies united.

The various representatives in Congress often talked of the troubles of *their* colony. Patrick Henry, of the Virginia delegation, saw the danger in this. He realized that self-interest could destroy the common effort. He stood up. His words rang out, "The distinctions between Virginians, Pennsylvanians, New Yorkers, and New Englanders are no more. I AM NOT A VIRGINIAN BUT AN AMERICAN!"

Chapter 4

ETHAN ALLEN, BENEDICT ARNOLD, AND FORT TICONDEROGA

PATRICK HENRY's remark was hated by the Tories.

It was no secret that the Tories and men in the British Army despised American fighting men. The Redcoats looked upon the Americans as worthless individuals—poor soldiers. A stiff fight was not expected from the American "cowards." One British general, Alured Clarke, said in England that he could control America if he were given one thousand British grenadiers. A member of the House of Commons, named Grant, went him one better. Colonel Grant said that he could march through all America with five regiments. Throughout the war, the British kept this attitude. Lieutenant Thomas Hughes, of the British Army, was captured by the Americans. After two years' imprisonment, Hughes said that the Americans "fawned like beaten spaniels." The British fighting men underestimated what Americans could do.

But the British governors in the colonies realized that aroused patriots were dangerous. When the news of Lexington and Concord spread about the land, many of the royal governors took refuge aboard British warships as fast as they could.

Now two Americans of undoubted courage came to the front:

Ethan Allen of Vermont and Benedict Arnold of Connecticut.

Ethan Allen was one of the most amazing of Americans. He was daring, ambitious, hard to control, and one of the strongest men in the mountain country between New Hampshire and New York. His physical strength was a frontier legend. It was said he could take a sack containing a bushel of salt, grip it in his teeth, and toss it over his head. People claimed to have seen Ethan bend iron nails in his fingers.

Ethan Allen was picturesque in dress. He often wore a buckskin jacket, homespun breeches, leather moccasins, with a tomahawk stuck in his belt. He loved to hunt, and his brother, Ira, said Ethan would run a deer down just to tire it out before he killed it. Ethan was also a great storyteller and at times used rough language. The unpopular British governor of New York put a price on Ethan's head because he did not like Ethan's conduct in a dispute about land. This increased Ethan's popularity in the Green Mountains. Allen had a sense of humor, and it did not worry him that Governor Tryon of New York had made him an outlaw.

At times Ethan Allen was cruel. For instance, in the dead of winter, he arranged for a minister who had complained to the governor to have a trial. The minister received two hundred lashes on his bare back as a result, then Ethan cheerfully gave him "free and unmolested passport to the City of New York."

Ethan Allen, his brothers, and Seth Warner organized the Green Mountain Boys and armed them. The idea was, Ethan said, to protect the land between New York and New Hampshire, known as "The Grants." Allen really meant that his famous band would fight rather than have the Grants become part of New York or New Hampshire.

Ethan's hatred for British ideas was reflected by his Green Mountain Boys, that is, by all except his brother, Levi. Levi *liked* Tory ideas. When war broke he left with Tories to make his home in Canada. Ethan appeared before the Bennington, Vermont, court and applied to have Levi's property sold for benefit of the state. When Levi heard of this, he challenged Ethan to a duel, but Ethan declined. He said, "It would be disgraceful to fight a Tory."

In May, 1775, teamed with Ethan Allen, the unusual leader from the Green Mountains, was a man of thirty-four who had the build of an athlete, a Roman nose, light eyes, a swarthy complexion, and great ambition. His name was Benedict Arnold.

Arnold had a hard background. His father was a wastrel, the town drunkard. Stories of Benedict Arnold's boyhood would be difficult to believe had he not eventually betrayed his country. These stories tell of young Arnold's horsewhipping school children at times and performing feats of peril to startle his friends. There was a gristmill at Norwich, Connecticut, and young Arnold liked to hang onto its wheel while it turned, half of the time being under water or in the falling torrent. He was a fine hand with rifle and pistol.

When trouble flared in the French and Indian War near Lake George, New York, fifteen-year-old Arnold ran away from home and enlisted. But he deserted and managed to evade recruiting officers sent to locate him. He became a successful druggist in New Haven and eventually a wealthy West Indian trader. He was not a man to trifle with, for he had become a husky fellow with a hot temper; he had fought two duels.

When Benedict Arnold heard the exciting news from Lexington and Concord, he formed a company. He was named its captain and at once demanded muskets, powder, and ball from the village selectmen at New Haven, and got them. He clapped on his tricornered hat, drew his sword, and marched his company toward the danger.

In Cambridge, Massachusetts, Captain Arnold proposed to the Committee of Public Safety that he be allowed to capture the

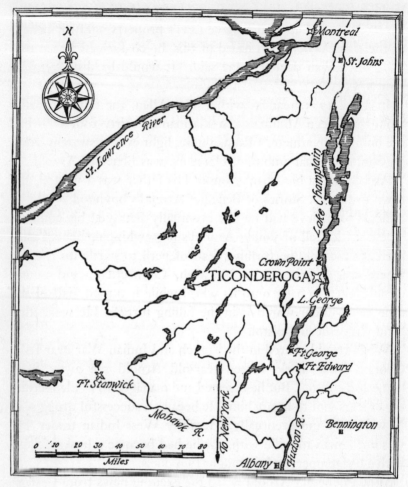

MAP No. 3

key British fortress of Ticonderoga. This was a twenty-year-old
fort situated on a high point of land jutting out into Lake Champlain. It was an important place, for whoever garrisoned the fort
controlled passage between Lake Champlain and Lake George.
For years these two lakes had been one of the principal routes

savages, renegades, and Frenchmen took when they came south to raid settlements in New York. Benedict persuaded the members of the committee that possession of the fort was vital. He also said he believed the fort held cannons and gunpowder, two supplies badly needed by the revolutionists.

About the same time, Ethan Allen of Vermont *also* decided Fort Ticonderoga should be captured. The news from Lexington and Concord inflamed him, too, and he wanted to fight somebody, somewhere, in order to help the cause. Fort Ticonderoga looked like a plum to Ethan, and when news came that Captain Arnold was going to attack it, Ethan persuaded the town fathers of Bennington, Vermont, to let him take the pick of the Green Mountain Boys and capture the fort. He felt nothing could stop his rugged Boys.

Ethan Allen looked imposing as he stood in the trees on the Vermont side, gazing at the fortress. He wore a green military coat, with bushy gold epaulets, and yellow breeches. About him stood one hundred and thirty of his Green Mountain Boys. They were in every kind of rough dress and carried almost every type of small arms. They were a motley crew. However, the leader's determination to win inspired them. "I think the best way to take the fort is by night attack," Ethan Allen told them.

Up marched an officer in a scarlet coat. This was Captain Benedict Arnold. Arnold produced papers showing his mission. He said he had volunteers from Massachusetts and Connecticut nearby. He expected to take command of the attack, but Ethan Allen had no intention of surrendering the lead. And the Green Mountain Boys said they would fight only if Ethan were the leader. Arnold gave in because he saw doing so was the only solution to taking the fort.

The two leaders crossed the water at night with eighty-three of their best men. On the New York shore Ethan addressed the raiders. He said the fame of the Green Mountain Boys had spread abroad, that in the attack he would be in the front rank, that the fighting would be desperate. He then gave anyone who wanted to go back a chance to do so. Not a man withdrew.

Ethan Allen and Benedict Arnold marched side by side as the little column marched down a dirt trail through the night toward the fort. The sleepy British sentry at the main gate was surprised. He managed to point his musket at the leaders, but it misfired. In rushed the raiders with wild yells. The sentry fled, Ethan Allen at his heels. They found the Officer of the Day's gate unlocked. Ethan hit the next sentry over the head with the flat of his sword and ordered him to show him the commandant's quarters, which the soldier did. Backed by a group of his men, Ethan shouted into a doorway, "Come out of there, you damned old rat!" A British lieutenant came out in his night dress and demanded what right Ethan had to be in the King's fort. Ethan held up his sword and yelled his answer, "In the name of the Great Jehovah and the Continental Congress!"

The commandant, Captain William Delaplane, surrendered his sword to Ethan and the fort rang with the cheers of the Americans. The prisoners were paraded, and then the Continentals broke into the commandant's supply of rum.

On May 10, 1775, the day Fort Ticonderoga's small garrison of two officers and forty-three men surrendered to Ethan Allen and Benedict Arnold, the Second Continental Congress met in Philadelphia. The fight at Lexington and Concord had its effect on these patriots, too. The congressmen were united by the common danger. They faced grave problems. The colonies expected to get their civil rights back and to determine the best way to live more harmoniously with Great Britain. Only the Loyalists were skeptical of success.

The Loyalists did not see how the thirteen tiny colonies could

stand against the greatest power on earth, and they thought it wrong even to consider doing so.

When Congress met, enthusiasm filled the air in Philadelphia. When Colonel George Washington and the Virginia delegation reached a point six miles from Philadelphia, they were received by a party of five hundred horsemen and escorted into town. A band also greeted the column and led the parade through the streets. Other delegations were met with bands and paraded. The town buzzed with excitement.

Peyton Randolph of Virginia was again elected president of the Congress. There were the same leaders, with a few exceptions, who had represented the colonies at the First Continental Congress nine months before. The famous patriot from Massachusetts, John Hancock, was a newcomer. So was Thomas Jefferson of Virginia. One of the strongest characters was the wealthy John Dickinson of Philadelphia, who hoped Congress could find a way to settle the difficulties without a war.

Sitting quietly watching the younger men was Ben Franklin, the best known and most famous American of the day. He had just returned from England. He was at the end of his patience with the English, for he had done his best to make the English leaders see the American side of the problem but he had not succeeded. Ben Franklin had even offered to pay for the tea thrown into Boston Harbor out of his own pocket. When he was in England he had heard ridiculous proposals as to how to bring the colonies "to their senses," such as the idea of burning every American seaport town. He also knew of the ridiculous light in which British military men regarded American fighting men. He had heard stories such as the one which arrived after Lexington and Concord, that a British sergeant had captured forty colonial soldiers and had marched them into Boston.

Franklin had even been offered a bribe to return to America in the British service, which, of course, he refused to accept. His family was, like many families in America, torn apart in its sympathies. His son, William, who lived in Perth Amboy, and was the governor of New Jersey for the Crown, believed that the cause of the colonies was wrong. But Benjamin Franklin did not agree; he was now signing his letters "B. Free Franklin."

Before Ben Franklin left England, a British nobleman who knew of Ben's wit asked him to write a fable. When paper and ink were put before him, Franklin decided to illustrate the times. He wrote about a strong eagle, sailing the sky, who had spied a hare and had darted down "like a sunbeam" and had seized the little creature in his claws. But the eagle had made a mistake; the "hare" was a cat. The cat, Franklin said, dug its claws into the eagle's breast and seized the bird's throat with its teeth. The eagle told the cat to let go its hold and that he would release it. But the cat had no desire to be crushed to death by a fall from such a height. "You have taken me up," said the cat, "and you shall let me down." This was Ben Franklin's idea of the situation between Great Britain and her colonies in America. In his mind, their fates interlaced; both would have to make sacrifices and concessions if they were to get along.

"Getting along"—knowing what to do—was difficult. An express rider galloped into Philadelphia bearing the news from Ethan Allen that "the Green Mountain Boys and soldiers from the Massachusetts Bay Colony" (as Ethan expressed it) had captured Fort Ticonderoga. Ethan made no mention of Benedict Arnold in his message to Congress.

The excitement over the capture of one of the King's forts shook the Congress. A number of proposals were made as to what to do with the fort and its supplies. For one thing, the fort needed repairs. But the delegates realized the value of the ten tons of musket balls, the one hundred and twenty cannons, barrels of powder, lead, flint, pork, beans, and other articles which were captured. But what colony owned these supplies, and who owned the fort?

Congress acted cautiously. It approved the capture of Fort Ticonderoga, saying that Great Britain was planning an attack from Canada. Then Congress recommended that New York move the cannon, powder, and other stores from the fort to the southern part of Lake George, where it could be returned to the Crown when there was a restoration of harmony.

In the meantime, up in the beautiful Lake Champlain country, the two military leaders, both jealous of each other, considered the next move. Benedict Arnold was disgusted with Ethan Allen and the Green Mountain Boys, whom he considered wild and undisciplined. Arnold believed he should be in command of Fort Ticonderoga, and that he was a better military leader than Allen. The Boys did not like Benedict Arnold and, on two occasions, shot at him.

The situation was tense until two Americans sailed up to the fort in command of a sloop and several bateaux which they had captured at the south end of Lake Champlain.

Benedict Arnold was given command of these vessels, probably because he was a sailor and because Ethan and the Green Mountain Boys knew nothing about ships. Arnold and his brave men captured the British fort at St. Johns on the Richelieu River, a small, sloop-rigged vessel, and valuable supplies. This was only thirty miles from Montreal.

Seth Warner, a Green Mountain Boy, captured Crown Point on Lake Champlain, not far from Fort Ti. Ethan sent word of the capture to Albany. Then he wrote *"We are in Want of Almost Every Necessary (Courage Excepted)...."*

While he listed his needs, Ethan also desired more fighting. He got an idea that if he established an advance post not far from St. Johns he would have a base from which he could make war on the Redcoats in Canada. He wanted the Indians to join him and he wrote the chiefs in the neighborhood, "I have always loved Indians and I have hunted a great deal with them and know how to shute and ambush just like an Indian.... I want your warriors to join with me and my warriors like brothers and ambush the Regulars. I will give you money, blankits, Tomehawks, Knives and Paint because they first killed our men when it was Peace time...."

However, this letter was intercepted and carried to the hands of the British governor in Canada, Sir Guy Carleton. But a greater blow was the message from Congress ordering Ethan to take the cannon and stores of Fort Ticonderoga to the southern end of Lake George, where they could be given back to the

King's representatives *when* there was "harmony." Ethan Allen was dumfounded. He urged an attack. He wrote Congress:

It is my humble opinion, that the more vigorous the Colonies push the war against the King's Troops in Canada the more friends we shall find in that Country. Should the colonies send an army of two or three thousand men and attack Montreal, we should have little to fear from the Canadians or Indians, and would easily make a conquest of that place. . . .

Ethan Allen underestimated the hardships of making war in Canada, but he knew more of the enemy situation than the majority of the leaders in Philadelphia. There was no chance for immediate restoration of harmony. There was no turning back.

Chapter 5

THE BATTLE OF BUNKER HILL

Two months after the fight at Lexington and Concord, the King dispatched more Redcoats to Boston. This meant there were sixty-five hundred soldiers ready to punish the Americans. With the new arrivals he sent three experienced major generals: William Howe, Henry Clinton, and John Burgoyne.

William Howe was a soldier of considerable reputation. He had been in the army since he was seventeen. When he was a young major in the French and Indian War, he bravely led the advance guard up the cliff at Quebec when Wolfe defeated the French general Montcalm on the Plains of Abraham. General William Howe was portly. He was not an energetic officer. Food, drink, and a gay time were the most important things in his life. But Howe had a way with troops. They liked him for he was approachable and he was not a stern disciplinarian.

General Henry Clinton had once served in the New York militia but had transferred to the British Army. He was a short, dumpy fellow, not inspiring to look at. But people discovered in the French and Indian War that Clinton could be counted upon to do his duty.

General John Burgoyne, sometimes called "Gentleman

Johnny," was a handsome, charming fellow. He was a hero of the Seven Years' War. Burgoyne was interested in caring for his men (which was unusual in any army at that time). But he was not one to issue unpopular orders, even if those orders were necessary to the success of the campaign. Gentleman Johnny Burgoyne was not loyal to Governor General Gage and did his best to undermine him in letters home.

When the three generals arrived in Boston and looked over the situation, Burgoyne said, "What! Ten thousand peasants keeping five thousand soldiers of the King shut in! Well, let us get in. We'll soon have elbow room."

General Gage, with the advice of the three generals, issued a proclamation, phrased in high-sounding words, branding everyone who had borne arms against the Crown, or who helped the rebels, as a traitor. However, all "except Samuel Adams and John Hancock" were promised pardon if they would lay down their arms and become peaceful again.

The Americans gave no answer in words. They replied by building breastworks on the night of June 16, 1775, on Breed's Hill near Charlestown, overlooking the city of Boston.

This was startling to the British Army, to the sailors on the men-of-war anchored in the harbor, and to the Tories in Boston. It was obvious that when the patriots got cannon they could shell the British ships near the town, and if the ships left, the British in Boston would be cut off. Even though the patriots had worked with pick and shovel to fortify Breed's Hill, Bunker Hill—which was higher—gave its name to the battle that was about to start.

Governor General Gage immediately called a council of war. Attending it were the three newly arrived generals and important naval officers from the King's warships. The generals were pleased, for they believed the patriots had stuck their heads into a trap. General Clinton pointed out that all that had to be done

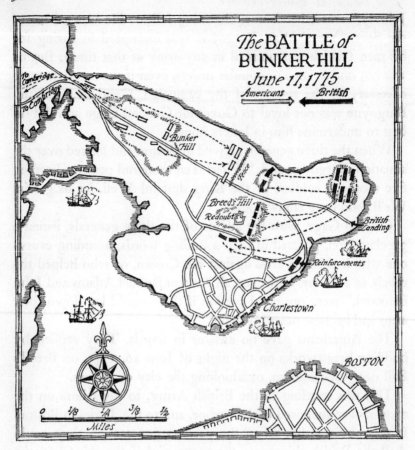

The BATTLE of
BUNKER HILL
June 17, 1775
Americans →   ← British

To Cambridge

Bunker
Hill

Breed's Hill
Redoubt

British
Landing

Reinforcements

Charlestown

BOSTON

0   1/8   1/4   3/8   1/2
Miles

MAP No. 4

was to land troops on the Neck and the Americans would be
captured. Warships could patrol the harbor and the New England Army on the hill would starve.

While this was the basis for a good plan, the council of war
did not like it. The council decided the best thing to do was to
land troops near Moulton's Hill and just march up and capture
the breastworks. A flanking movement from the north would be
necessary with a straight-on attack to hold the Americans. There

was no doubt that when the rebels saw the might of the British Army they would give up.

Working hard on the American side was a well-known character, General Israel Putnam. There were as many stories going around about Putnam as there were about Ethan Allen. Putnam, a heavy-set, muscular fellow, had established his fearlessness when, at the age of twenty-one, he had entered the den of a she-wolf that had slain seventy of his sheep and goats. With a rope around his waist, Putnam had crawled sixteen feet into a cave only two feet high. In one hand he held a torch, in the other his gun. He shot the wolf and he was hauled backward by friends on the other end of the rope to keep from being suffocated. Later, he re-entered the cave to make certain the monster was dead.

Israel Putnam had commanded a company in the French and Indian War and had gone on scouts in and near enemy camps with the famous Ranger, Major Robert Rogers. In fact, when Rogers had been taken prisoner by a Frenchman at the point of a weapon, Putnam had rescued Major Rogers by a hand-to-hand attack on the Frenchman. Everyone knew how Putnam had, in 1757, saved the powder magazine at Fort Edward when fire threatened three hundred barrels of powder. Putnam wore gloves made of blankets in accomplishing this deed; the gloves and his flesh were badly burned. He had been tortured and tomahawked by the Indians, but he had always managed to escape. On one scout, Putnam was captured, stripped naked, and lashed to a stake. The savages kindled a fire around him with the idea of roasting him alive. It looked like the end of a brave fighter, but a French officer named Molang came to his rescue and saved Putnam. "Old Put" was taken to General Montcalm in Montreal as a prisoner, and later exchanged.

Putnam was fifty-seven years old when the British attacked at Concord. As soon as he got the news of the battle, Israel Putnam hitched up a team of horses and drove one hundred miles from his Connecticut home to Cambridge, where he offered his services. He was one of America's best small-unit leaders, but he was not an outstanding general officer because he did not have the training or know-how to plan military operations.

Another American general, General Artemas Ward, sent word encouraging the diggers working in the night to fortify Breed's Hill.

But American leaders were not taking good care of their men. No one had seen that rations were on hand for breakfast and there was little water on the position. The day breaking was red hot and the patriots were tired after their night's work. A few deserted, but the majority of the two thousand men stood their ground, determined to keep the hill. British warships started raking the position with fire. The patriots could see barges loaded with Redcoats shove off from Boston and land at Moulton's Point and on the beaches of Charlestown, not far away. Colonel William Prescott, one of the bravest patriots present, took off his coat and got ready to fight. He was the principal leader in the fight which was about to start. With Old Put he moved along the line and steadied the men.

Across the water in Boston, throngs of people turned out to watch the battle. They occupied every vantage point and lined the shores. They expected to see the British Army walk over the Americans. The Tories were anxious to see the patriots punished. The Tories looked forward to peace and obedience to the King's law.

Snare drums rattled as the famous British light infantry crawled out of the barges and formed on the beaches less than a half-mile from the American fighters. The British grenadiers took their places. General Howe, himself, took position at the head of the formation. The British were dressed as for parade: red coats and white breeches, but someone had neglected to have them drop their heavy packs. They were to climb the steep hill and fight in the face of enemy fire with each soldier carrying an eighty-pound pack containing equipment such as a blanket, extra clothing, and food.

General Howe ordered his artillery to fire at the American breastworks. He waved his sword in the direction of the hill, and the Redcoats marched upward. The drums beat time as the Redcoats endeavored to keep their lines. Onward they came—slowly. The Americans held their fire until "they could see the white of their eyes." Then the volleys crashed, and brave English soldiers went down.

When the black smoke cleared, the watchers in Boston could see the British moving *back*—down the slope. The Tory watchers could hardly believe their eyes. The city of Charlestown burst into flames—a terrible backdrop to a horrible scene. The wounded lying in front of the American position were crying for help.

The British re-formed and attacked again, over their dead and wounded.

Again the American fire tore the British ranks apart, and the British retreated. General Howe had blood on his breeches. Everyone on his staff had been killed or wounded.

General Putnam galloped about on horseback. He raced across the Neck through fire from the warships to try to get reinforcements, but failed. Back he came, through the same shower of iron, to the top of the hill. He stopped for a moment to speak to Joseph Warren, a valuable patriot leader who had been promoted to general yet was fighting, by his own choice, as a private.

Below, the Redcoats were being reinforced by five hundred soldiers and marines. They had dropped their packs. They were coming back.

The situation on the hill was desperate, for each man now had less than a gill of powder.

On came the British. They were led by a teen-age lieutenant,

his sword at a salute. Brave General Howe, on his horse, was also at the front of the formation.

Again the patriots held their fire. When the range was close, the patriots fired. But the Redcoats swept over the position. The Americans left. It was the Redcoats' turn to mow down their enemy. One hundred and forty Americans fell dead, among them General Warren, who had been one of the last to leave the hill. The slopes were dotted with two hundred and twenty-six dead Redcoats. The British soon returned to Boston with their wounded and sent back for loads of dead.

The Tories were stunned. Bunker Hill was a British victory, but what a victory! The King could ill afford such costly wins over the American "farmers." The Tories were amazed that many green American troops had remained on the position and had fought bravely.

Soon, violence broke out elsewhere against the hated Tories. In New York, a troop of horsemen rode to the shop of a printer who supported the Loyalist cause. They broke his presses and carried off his type. Tories were ridden on rails, and in one instance a Loyalist woman was carried about on a rail by patriot women. In South Carolina, Georgia, in parts of Pennsylvania and Connecticut, the patriots clashed with Tories in civil war. These were not large battles, but they were bitter ones. Many Tories were thrown into jail and their property was stolen or destroyed.

In Boston, the Tories were better off, although life was hard. One patriot in Boston wrote, "We have pork and beans one day, beans and pork the next, and fish when we can catch it." But the British Army was there, and the Tories of Boston were safe for the time being.

Chapter 6

GENERAL GEORGE WASHINGTON

BEFORE the Battle of Bunker Hill, the congressmen seated in Philadelphia worried about what to do about the New England army. They realized that a collection of partially trained militia was not enough; that to beat England would require an organized, well-trained army. The congressmen puzzled over this and also over the problem of whom to appoint as commander in chief.

John Hancock was now president of the Congress. At a long meeting, Hancock sat back in his chair and listened to the chubby-faced John Adams discuss the problem. John Hancock, the wealthiest man in Massachusetts, expected his name would be put up for the post. Hancock had commanded a company of militia in the days when a crack company escorted the royal governor on formal occasions. He was prominent in the rebellion against England. Everyone knew how his ship, *The Liberty*, had been seized as a smuggler by the Crown, and how Hancock had used that to dramatize the plight of the colonies. John Hancock felt he deserved the job.

But John Adams did not nominate John Hancock, and the meeting adjourned.

44

In the taverns and inns, the congressmen talked of old Artemas Ward, who had been a colonel in the French and Indian days and who was keeping the militia together up at Boston. But word had come that General Ward did not want to be senior general of the proposed army.

Another "candidate" was Major General Charles Lee, a sour-looking man, so thin he appeared to be sick. Charles Lee had had an amazing career. He had been an officer since he was *eleven*, when he received his first commission in His Majesty's service. Lee was ambitious, headstrong, and vain. He had an acid tongue and a fiery temper, and Thomas Johnson of Maryland warned the other congressmen that Lee could not be trusted.

In his career, Lee had fought several duels. He had learned Indian fighting from experts: the Mohawk Indians, who had given him the name of "Boiling Water." He was that kind of man—Boiling Water was a good name for Charles Lee.

Lee had been wounded leading Englishmen in General Abercromby's rash, suicide attacks at Fort Ticonderoga in the French and Indian War. He had fought in Portugal and had served in Poland. He had been the King's ambassador to Turkey, and had fought bandits at the head of a band of Cossacks in Russia. He was ambitious to become a British general, but along the way his sharp tongue and his pen had made too many enemies. He came to America three years before the fight at Lexington and Concord and had declared himself vigorously on the side of the patriots. He had a hatred now for the British; he resigned his commission in their army, and some of his property in England had been destroyed as a result. But Charles Lee had little chance of being named commander in chief, although he was in Philadelphia and was available, for the congressmen desired to pick a man of American birth.

The next day, in the beautiful meeting room in the State House, John Adams talked again about the importance of selecting the right man. He discussed George Washington, an erect colonel of Virginia militia, six feet two inches tall, who sat by the door. Washington was forty-three and looked younger in his trim buff and blue uniform. He had powdered hair (like the men of his station and time), blue-gray eyes, and a ruddy face which had been marked by smallpox.

Almost every man present in the State House knew how young Washington had been employed as surveyor on Lord Fairfax's five-million-acre tract west of the Blue Ridge; how he had been selected by Governor Dinwiddie of Virginia to travel through the wilderness to a French fort on the shores of Lake Erie with an order for the French to withdraw. It was common knowledge how young Washington had proven his bravery with General Braddock when that British general had had his command torn to shreds by the French and Indians. On that occasion Washington had two horses shot beneath him and six bullet holes had pierced his coat.

The Virginia delegation knew even more about George Washington. They knew he had been born in the first rank of colonial society; that he was a serious-minded businessman, a scientific farmer who owned fifty thousand acres; that he had become a member of the Virginia House of Burgesses at the age of twenty-seven; and that he had married Martha Custis. They knew he had a fine brain, that he was moral, obstinate, very sensitive, and that he hid his sense of humor. They realized that he had steel and devotion to duty in his make-up, and that he could inspire men. They also felt he was ambitious. Washington was prepared to accept the job before the debate started. He had made his last will since arriving in Philadelphia and had purchased five military textbooks and had been studying to learn everything he could about military life.

When John Adams's remarks about his record became embarrassing, George Washington stood up, straight as an Indian, and slipped out of the room.

Congress voted to adopt the New England army and to build it as best they could. The date was June 14, 1775, the birthday still remembered by our army.

John Adams talked on. He emphasized that *George Washington* was the man who could bring the colonists together. He ended his speech by nominating "the beloved Colonel Washington," and Sam Adams seconded the motion. These were decisions that affected the entire course of the war. Washington accepted the position. When he was told his pay would be five hundred dollars a month, he replied he would keep a record of his expenses and collect them instead of a salary.

As soon as he could select his staff, General George Washington prepared to leave for Boston. He rode off to war with an impressive farewell, passing through long lines of congressmen and citizens who turned out to wish him God's speed. Near him rode the adventurer, Major General Charles Lee, whom Washington had chosen as a staff officer. It proved to be an unwise choice.

When George Washington and his staff officers had ridden several hours out of Philadelphia on their way to Boston, they met an express rider bearing news of Bunker Hill. Washington was impressed when he heard that the patriots had made such a wonderful stand against the Redcoats, but he did not realize that a myth would arise from that battle. The people would believe for a long time that untrained militia were equal to trained, disciplined troops. It was a myth Washington and others had to labor hard to correct.

All along his trip north crowds turned out to greet Washington. The people believed him to be the outstanding military leader of the colonies and they were right, but few realized the tremendous difficulties in the path ahead of him.

Thirteen days later, George Washington rode beneath a huge

elm upon the Common at Cambridge. It was July 3, 1775. In front of him were lined the available troops. George Washington drew his sword and took command of the Continental Army. It was a moment that thrilled the patriots, and to the new commander in chief it brought realization of the tremendous task he faced. His army was in miserable shape, and he had the problem of keeping the British in Boston until he was able to drive them out.

Washington inspected his fifteen thousand men. He felt ill when he saw the army. He was horrified by the filthy huts in which the men lived and by their lack of uniforms. Many men wore a mixture of military and civilian dress, others wore the rough woolen clothing of the frontier. The officers did not even know how many men they had, for there were no rosters, or lists. The supply of powder was dangerously low—if the ammunition were distributed equally, there would be less than *nine* rounds per man—and the enemy was just across the Neck in Boston.

Many patriot soldiers hated to obey orders. They, generally, were individualists. They felt little need of discipline. They did not see why they could not do as they pleased as long as it was morally right. If a soldier was imprisoned for an offense, his friends in ranks might break open the jail and free him. Some officers controlled their men very well; others did not.

George Washington started to work. He gave certain men the task of getting food for the army. He asked Congress to furnish better uniforms. And he recommended to the congressmen that certain officers be appointed generals. This caused jealousies, but it did not stop him. He made officers submit correct lists of their men, so he would know exactly how many men he had. It took eight days to carry out this order! He made the soldiers drill, for he wanted them to learn how to maneuver and how to obey. He gave orders to reduce drinking, swearing, and to observe the Sabbath. He set the example by going to church. He knew gambling would cause trouble, so he published this order:

GENERAL ORDERS

Head Quarters
October, 3, 1775

Any officer; non Commission'd Officer, or Soldier, who shall be detected playing at Toss-up, pitch and hustle, or any other Games of chance, in or near Camp or Villages bordering on the encampments; shall without delay be confined and punished for disobedience of orders.

The patriot army began to look less like a mob.

The army discovered that its head general was mentally prepared. Both officers and men felt his powerful personality. Washington inspired the officers to become better leaders. The army gained confidence.

Soon Congress managed to send Washington reinforcements. One of the first groups to arrive were sharpshooters from Virginia. Their leader was the gigantic Captain Dan Morgan. Morgan had worked as a teamster under General Braddock twenty years before, and his back bore the scars of the cat-o'-nine-tails.

Captain Dan Morgan was a natural leader. He knew his men and how to get the best from them. They were dressed in fringed buckskin trousers, moccasins, and green hunting shirts. Powder horns and shot bags were slung over their shoulders. Many wore black hats that rose to a peak in front. Deertails were fastened to the side, and yellow bands painted on the top of the hats bore the word: CONGRESS. Dan Morgan and his sharpshooters were anxious to do their share. To report to General Washington, they traveled six hundred miles in twenty-one days.

Washington soon put men on the job of finding powder. This involved commissioning a fleet of privately owned ships called "privateers." The idea was for these ships to intercept British vessels bringing supplies to America—to capture the vessels and their cargoes. "Washington's fleet" worked hard. It soon captured over thirty ships flying the British Union Jack, and the supplies they brought in were a godsend to the Continental Army. One enemy supply ship yielded one hundred thousand flints, two thousand small arms, and thirty-two tons of lead balls. Other captured ships furnished food for the patriot army.

One of the biggest headaches confronting the new commander in chief was the custom of short-term enlistments. Some militiamen were serving under a five-month term (and many of these men had gone home). Others were serving for eight months. The general wondered how he could fight, with his men constantly coming and going. To encourage enlistments, some colonies had bonuses called "bounties," but the bounties were not the same in each colony. For example, Rhode Island rewarded a man who enlisted with an extra month's pay, plus a knapsack and blanket; Massachusetts gave a bounty of a coat, a blanket, and a small sum of money.[1]

The bounty system helped, but the problem of men enlisting for such short periods worried Washington. He knew it was a custom in the colonies for a man to serve only for short periods of time. The system enabled a man to return home after serving several months, so he could see his family and help with the crops or other work. This was fine, but it was not the way to win a war; and Washington realized it. He asked Congress to make the term of enlistment one year. Even this period proved too short. It would have been far better to have men enlist for the duration of the war.

Punishments in armies of the times were severe. Numbers of officers were tried by court-martial and dismissed. Men were punished by being made to sit in the stocks, run on a barrel top,

---

[1] Late in 1776, Congress fixed the bounty at twenty dollars, a suit of clothes, and one hundred acres of land.

or to "rest" for hours sitting on a sharp sawhorse. Under the law, the maximum number of lashes a man could receive for a crime was thirty-nine. Washington wrote Congress this was not enough, and Congress increased the number to one hundred.

Gradually the American Army began to take shape, and the British in Boston obliged by doing little. They staged some raids, cannonading, and that was all. When General Israel Putnam watched the British fire cannon balls at the American lines facing Boston, the old general offered a small glass of rum for each cannon ball recovered. Men chased cannon balls bounding across the landscape, in hopes they would be duds and not explode, or that they could reach them and snuff out the fuses before they blew up. A number of men lost arms and legs in this dangerous way of getting ammunition.

Word came to the Continental Army that a British naval captain, Henry Mowat, had landed in Falmouth (later Portland), Maine, and had burned over three hundred buildings in the town, including the library, church, and courthouse. And winter was not far away!

Then the evil and untrustworthy British governor of Virginia, the Earl of Dunmore, gave the biggest seaport in his colony, the town of Norfolk, a New Year's Day "present." He arranged for seamen from British men-of-war to shoot red-hot shot into the town and at the forces of the Virginia patriots. Soon, hundreds of homes were in flames. Most of Norfolk burned when patriots themselves set fire to buildings. They did this because so many Tories lived in the town.

When Washington's army heard the terrible news from Maine and Virginia, even more hatred developed.

The Continental Army had the British penned up in Boston and the British were in a bad situation. They had few supplies, many wounded who were not receiving adequate care, and a great number of sick.

George Washington realized it was a good time to attack, but he lacked cannon. His artillery chief made a suggestion. His name was Henry Knox, and he was outstanding in more ways than one. He weighed two hundred and sixty pounds and towered even above Washington. Colonel Knox was a man people liked to have around because he possessed enthusiasm and brains. Young Knox told the general he could go to Fort Ticonderoga, get the big guns there, and bring them back.

Not everyone believed this was a good plan. It was the middle of November, 1775, and the weather was getting colder. It meant a round trip of two hundred and fifty miles, and part of it through the Berkshire Mountains. Where there were no trails, Knox and his cannoneers would have to cut their own.

But Washington approved the idea and told Knox it was imperative he bring the guns back.

Knox had a fine background. He knew engineering and he loved books, and from books he studied artillery and tactics. In peacetime, Knox had owned a bookstore in Boston. When war came, he sold his store and left Boston to fight for liberty. He knew he would never get his bookstore back in the condition in which he had left it. This was the man Washington felt could do this important job.

After Knox left on his mission, Washington sent spies, whom he paid out of his own pocket, into Boston to learn about the British. The spies estimated there were about ten thousand "lobsters" there, and more were expected from England.

Washington began to worry. When more British troops came, no doubt the enemy would break out. If he had cannon he could bombard the Redcoats, but he did not know when Henry Knox would come back; perhaps Knox would not be able to make it at all. Washington thought of attacking across the Boston Harbor ice, but the ice was not strong enough. The general ordered the patriots to build two floating batteries and forty-five barges, but he did not relish a landing in the face of the enemy.

A month passed, then two. No sign of Colonel Knox. Finally, word came that Henry Knox was at Framingham, twenty miles west of Cambridge, with forty-three cannon and sixteen mortars. Knox and his men had placed the guns on heavy sleds and used oxen to do the pulling. It had been a journey in which the knowledge of engineering and the leadership of Knox paid off. Several times a heavy cannon crashed through the ice of a river or lake and sank. But Knox and his company did not lose a gun. They had a difficult time in the snowy Berkshires with their load of 119,900 pounds of iron. Their reward was that they arrived in time for Washington to use the cannon against the Redcoats.

In Boston, on an evening in October, 1775, the British General Burgoyne was attending a play in Boston which made fun of the patriots. It was called *The Blockade of Boston*, and the general himself had written it. One of the actors, dressed like a Yankee sergeant, suddenly appeared at the center of the stage and cried, "*Silence!* The alarm guns have been fired! A battle is going on in Charlestown!" There was great applause and then wild confusion. The audience panicked and ran out. They thought a general attack was occurring.

Now in March, 1776, George Washington did attack. He secretly mounted the cannon from Ticonderoga on Dorchester Heights. The big mortar, "Old Sow," roared and a thirteen-inch cannon ball arced into the British lines. The target was the British position. Both Redcoats and Tories were surprised. Immediately, seamen on the men-of-war in the harbor began to worry, for they were "sitting ducks" which could be sunk by cannon fire. The ships moved quickly out of range.

The Tories were terrified. They had looked to the Redcoats for protection and now, with cannon balls ripping the city apart, the British were talking of evacuating—that is, moving

away as fast as they could. The British cannon fired back, but they were not in as good positions as the American guns on the hills. More than eight hundred cannon balls tore through the city. The noise could be heard for miles.

One patriot wrote in his diary, "There was afireing of Bums all night and they killed one man at Litchmors point with a Bum."

Confusion and pillaging broke out in Boston. It was everyone for himself. British soldiers broke into homes and stores and wrecked them, taking what they wanted.

Word filtered out of the city that the Redcoats were saying that General Howe was taking them north to Halifax. Shortly, the British rounded up schooners, sloops, barkentines, every available type of ship which might weather a blow at sea. The Redcoats got aboard, and with them went more than one thousand Tories. The British surprised the patriots by leaving behind many cannon and many war supplies.

General Washington wondered if the movement of the enemy was a trick. He had experienced trickery in war when he had fought Indians. Why should the British sail for Halifax? It seemed more logical to him that they should sail for New York, the principal port of the colonies.

The enemy fleet hung around Nantucket, off the coast. Finally, it sailed out to sea. Where it had gone, no American knew for sure.

George Washington left at once with most of his army to defend New York City. The spirit in the Continental Army was up. The troops now believed in General Washington. They liked his idea that they should consider themselves a band of brothers, willing and ready to die for each other. They would need this spirit, for harder days lay ahead.

Chapter 7

THE ATTACK ON CANADA

WHILE Washington had the British cooped up in Boston, many colonists worried for fear the Canadians would strike southward from Montreal. It was pointed out they could take Fort Ticonderoga and then travel the old invasion route: southward along Lake Champlain and Lake George, then down the Hudson River. People also said the British might use Indians, as the French had several years before.

The ambitious Benedict Arnold reassured Congress by saying that if he had two thousand men he could turn the tables by capturing Montreal and Quebec. News from the north was favorable to this idea. John Brown, a Massachusetts lawyer, had been on a secret mission to Montreal and Quebec. Brown was an adventurer, and a trip as dangerous as this in the dead of winter appealed to him. He came back from his journey and said all that was needed was an attack on Canada, that many Canadians were anxious to help. This jibed with Ethan Allen's enthusiastic message to Congress. The chances of Canada becoming the fourteenth colony looked excellent. The Americans felt the time had come for conquest.

But the British governor in Canada, Guy Carleton, was work-

MAP No. 5

ing hard. To aid him, Bishop Briand ordered the rites of the church denied any Roman Catholic who gave help to the colonies. But not every Catholic in Canada accepted this. They felt the bishop was acting like a general rather than a bishop. Even the country people, who had great faith, began to wonder where the line was between the church and politics.

After thinking over all the proposals for an attack on Canada, General Washington decided upon a two-pronged invasion. One force would strike Montreal; the other, Quebec.

But how many men could Washington spare for the expeditions? With the British just across the Neck in Boston, he hesitated to reduce his army. Finally, twenty-five hundred men started north up the old invasion route under General Richard Montgomery.

Colonel Benedict Arnold would lead eleven hundred others up the Kennebec River.

Such small forces made the attack on the Canadians a rash gamble; but the stakes were high, for if the Americans could take the two towns, Canada might become American forever.

Richard Montgomery was an Irishman with a face like a Greek statue. He had been a captain in the British Army and, when the British captured Quebec sixteen years before, this genial but forceful Irishman had been a friend of the man he would now attack, General Carleton. With General Montgomery was the wild mountain leader, Ethan Allen.

When Montgomery and his twenty-five hundred men arrived at the enemy's wooden fort on the Richelieu River at St. Johns, they halted. It was a low fort, almost at the water's edge and surrounded by a ditch in which obstacles had been placed. General Montgomery wisely decided he could not leave a fort containing six hundred men in his rear. If he did, the enemy would follow him and would also capture any supplies and messages sent to him. Yet the general did not desire to attack the fort because it would cost him too many men—men he would need in Quebec when he joined with Benedict Arnold. So Montgomery lay siege to the fort and bombarded it. He also sent a scouting force ahead under Ethan Allen and John Brown.

But things were not simple for Montgomery even though he had an enemy cooped in a large wooden box. The American soldiers were not well disciplined. They thought, *If we are fighting for freedom, why are we taking orders, obeying General Montgomery's slightest whim?* They did not see that an army has no time for elections and every man cannot be a general. These were not the kind of troops General Montgomery had been used to in the British Army, and he almost went home. It took patience on his part to lead undisciplined soldiers.

He next had trouble with food and powder supply, sickness, and desertion. And bad news came from Ethan Allen. When Ethan was on his own, he decided to startle the world by capturing Montreal. But he ran into Canadians. It was one hundred of Ethan's men against one thousand of the enemy and, after a fight, Ethan and forty of his men were captured.

The British were delighted to have as their prisoner one of the leaders of the rebellion—a man who had helped capture Fort Ticonderoga. General Prescott, the Britisher in Montreal, roared when Ethan was brought before him, "You will grace a halter at Tyburn!" Ethan knew what that meant. Tyburn was the place in England where criminals were hanged.

Ethan was handcuffed, and his legs were shackled to a long thirty-pound bar. His next berth was the dank hold of a ship bound for England. He was starved and treated miserably, but he was not hanged; he was imprisoned. Ethan Allen was out of the war for a while.

Losing Ethan was a blow to General Montgomery, but the general turned his attention to another fort not far from St. Johns, which he captured. This gave him control of the Richelieu. He continued to pour mortar fire into Fort St. Johns. While Montgomery was having his troubles, things were much worse inside the fort, where the garrison was on half rations. Finally the fort surrendered, although there were three days' rations left.

To capture Fort St. Johns, Richard Montgomery had taken fifty-five days. Valuable time, for his main mission was to get on to Quebec. Now there was an unusual spectacle: a mutiny. His troops became sullen and angry because they could not have the reserve supply of British clothing they found inside the fort.

The general had promised it to the enemy. It took much talking on the general's part to make his soldiers behave.

General Montgomery and his men pressed on when more help arrived. In two more weeks Montreal fell. More men went home without permission, and Montgomery was also forced to leave troops in Montreal to protect his rear. He marched on to Quebec through snow and over icy trails *with only three hundred men,* to meet Benedict Arnold.

Benedict Arnold's mission to march through the Maine wilderness would result in his soldiers facing danger, famine, and desertion. It would be one of the hardest campaigns in the history of the American Army. Few marches would require such endurance and fortitude.

The perilous nature of the mission appealed to the reckless spirit of Benedict Arnold. He was anxious to go. While he was not familiar with the route, he knew Quebec, for he had traded there when he was in civilian life. He also knew the obstacles he would face when he ordered an attack against the fortified town on the heights above the St. Lawrence. There was at hand for Arnold's study a map of the route made by Captain John Montresor of the British Army, who had made the trip fifteen years before. This map, while it gave an idea of the troubles and danger ahead, was carelessly made.

After a month of getting ready, Arnold's men sailed on ten transports to the mouth of the Kennebec River. A few miles below Fort Western (now Augusta), he went to a shipyard and inspected two hundred bateaux, flat-bottom boats, which he had previously ordered. He was greatly disappointed. The bateaux had been made in a rush with green lumber, and many were poorly put together. At this time, rumors came that Indian scouts were on the trail ahead; that they had been placed there by General Carleton to spy on the Americans. This did not bother Arnold. He divided his force into four parts, sending the rugged Daniel Morgan and his Virginia sharpshooters ahead to clear out the Indians.

Half a mile up the river from Fort Western were falls which required the men to take their heavy bateaux out of the water and carry them by hand. A portage, or "carry," on a river trip is a serious thing, for boats have to be unloaded, and supplies and then the boats carried to a place where the boats can be reloaded and put back into the water. It means much walking and hard labor, and usually, in the wilderness, the trails around carries were not worthy of the name.

When the bateaux were placed back in the river, there were

rapids to fight, and swift, white water. Arnold's men were experiencing the hardest kind of work. Now men began to get sick. Dr. Senter of Pennsylvania, marching at the end of the last group, had work to do to take care of those who became ill. He wrote in his journal:

Oct. 5, 1775 . . . By this time, many of our batteaux were nothing but wrecks, some stove to pieces, &c. The carpenters were employed in repairing them. . . . The dry cod fish lying loose in the batteaux, and being continually washed with fresh water running into the batteaux. The bread casks not being waterproof, admitted the water in plenty, burst the casks, as well as soured the bread. . . . Our fare was now reduced to salt pork and flour.
Oct. 11 . . . Decamped at the usual time, viz., at the rising sun. The water still continuing rapid. Our army now scattered up and down the road for a distance of ten or twelve miles. At 7 in the evening we quit the water, and with the greatest difficulty made a fire.
Oct. 12 . . . [Arrived at] the Great Carrying Place. . . . twelve mile [carry]. . . .
Oct. 14 . . . The army was now much fatigued, being obliged to carry all the batteaux, barrels of provisions, warlike stores, &c. Sometimes in mud knee deep, then over ledgy hills. . . .

The country became even more desolate. The bogs and the land about them looked like another planet.

Arnold now made a grave mistake. He sent letters by two Indians to friends in Quebec, telling them about the expedition. The Indians went to Quebec and gave the letters to Canadian officials. This was the first the Canadians knew of the expedition toiling through the wilderness, and they began to get ready to fight.

The weather got colder; ice formed in the streams. Many men were forced to turn back because of sickness, and the sick and the feeble lacked adequate food. The only shelter was afforded by the upturned bateaux on the wet banks. Some men deserted.

Arnold called a council of war of the leaders. He pointed out that, if the expedition continued, there was a chance of starvation. The leaders knew General Washington had given Arnold instructions to turn back if the trip seemed hopeless. But the trip did not seem hopeless to Arnold. He put the question to the council of war and the council voted to push on.

Now Lieutenant Colonel Roger Enos and one hundred and fifty men went home without permission and this discouraged those who remained.

The weather became even colder. There were two women on the expedition, the wife of a sergeant and the wife of a rifleman. Warner, a rifleman, gave out. When he could go no farther, he lay down under a tree. His wife took care of him as best she could and stayed with him until he died. She was unable to bury him, but covered him with leaves and hiked on to catch up with the rest of the expedition.

It now began to snow, and the storm lasted three days. When the exhausted men reached the end of the boggy country at the headwaters of the Kennebec River, a heartbreaking search began for the beginnings of the Chaudière River. The men hauled the heavy bateaux over rocky mountains; the compass direction was west-northwest. Dr. Senter wrote: *"Nov. 1st . . .* [We are eating] shaving soap, leather of shoes, cartridge boxes, &c., . . . a dog [belonging to a soldier] was devoured."

On November 2, the lives of the men were saved by friendly Canadians, who fed them. Benedict Arnold now had only six hundred and seventy-five men, who were in an exhausted, wretched condition.

The "army" plunged on to Quebec through the snows, in below-freezing weather. When they arrived opposite Quebec on the St. Lawrence, Arnold had scaling ladders made for the attack and he ordered his men to search the riverbank for canoes and small craft.

The Americans crossed the river at night, one of the birch bark canoes collapsing in the middle of the river. The occupants of the unlucky canoe were saved but were almost frozen to death.

Colonel Arnold and his men attacked Quebec but did not succeed. Soon after this, smallpox reduced the number in the American Army.

On December 2, General Montgomery joined Benedict Arnold at Quebec. The total American force was only 1,675.

Benedict Arnold sent a white flag forward to the walled city, demanding its surrender, but the Canadians fired a cannon at the messenger. General Montgomery tried three times to get the British governor, Carleton, to surrender, even sending his second letter by a woman to make sure it got through the enemy lines. But the letters failed to frighten General Carleton.

On the snowy night of December 31, 1775, the two American leaders and their men attacked the walled city, first striking the lower town. The bells in the town rang and drums were beaten, calling every available man to defense.

Arnold, Montgomery, and Daniel Morgan were everywhere, leading their men in a fearful night attack. The lower town was carried. A few more men and the Americans might have taken the upper town. General Montgomery was killed near the walls of the city and Arnold suffered a bad leg wound. The Americans were defeated, and six months later General Carleton drove them back across the river.

Arnold's march is one of the great marches in history. He and the Americans with him gave a demonstration of courage. But the invasion of Canada ended in dismal failure. The Americans were humiliated.

Chapter 8
THE DECLARATION OF INDEPENDENCE

THE months dragged by—hard months for the three principal groups of Americans: the patriots, a large middle group whose loyalties were undecided, and the Tories.

The British Parliament announced that Britain was at war with her colonies. Yet Congress had not taken a firm stand.

At this time, Tom Paine, a young author who wore his black hair in a "pigtail" after the fashion of the day, wrote a pamphlet which he called *Common Sense*. One hundred thousand copies of Paine's pamphlet sold in six months. Everywhere in the colonies people quoted Paine's stirring words. George Washington ordered parts of the pamphlet read to the army. Tom Paine's writing made many see the wisdom of separating from England.

Paine could manufacture phrases. It was he who first coined the words "UNITED STATES OF AMERICA."

Several things made Congress act: Paine's pamphlet; the decision of Parliament that the war was on; the burning of Falmouth, Maine; the cruel work of the Earl of Dunmore at Norfolk; the battles in Massachusetts; the fact that General Clinton had sailed with his Redcoats to spread the fighting to South Carolina; the knowledge that the King was hiring German soldiers to bring to America; and the appearance of British warships on blockade duty along the American coast.

It was obvious that the "old days" under the Crown were gone.

In 1775, Patrick Henry ended a speech in Richmond, Virginia, with words men could not forget, "Give me liberty or give me death."

A year later, many Americans believed the time had arrived to declare themselves, to state how they felt. At the Second Continental Congress, Richard Henry Lee of Virginia got up. He was an eloquent speaker who had been educated in England. He made a resolution which echoed Tom Paine's thoughts. "I move," Lee said, "that these united colonies ought to be free and independent...."

John Adams, too, talked for independence. "Sink or swim," he said, "live or die, survive or perish."

A committee was appointed in Congress to draft a paper telling how the colonies felt. The paper was largely the work of one man, Thomas Jefferson, one of the great Americans of history. This important paper declared Americans were free and had formed a *United States of America*. The Declaration was the birth of the United States.

Congress fixed the course. On July 4, 1776, the Declaration of Independence was adopted unanimously. The effect on the people was electric.

John Adams wrote his daughter from Philadelphia about the first Fourth of July celebration:

Yesterday, being the anniversary of the American Independence was celebrated here....

Congress determined to adjourn over the day, and to dine together. The general officers and others in town were invited.

In the morning the *Delaware* frigate, several large gallies, and other continental vessels, the Pennsylvania ship and guard boats, were all hawled off in the river, and several of them beautifully dressed in the colors of all nations, displayed about upon the masts, yards and rigging.

... we were saluted by a discharge of thirteen guns, which was followed by thirteen others, from each armed vessel in the river. The wharves and shores were lined with a vast concourse of people, all shouting and huzzaing, in a manner which gave great joy to every friend to this country, and the utmost terror and dismay to every lurking Tory.

At three we went to dinner ... good cheer, fine music ... continual volleys between every toast. ... The toasts were in honor of our country, and the heroes who have fallen. After this, two troops of lighthorse, raised in Maryland, accidentally here on their way to camp were paraded through Second Street, after them a train of artillery, and then about a thousand infantry from North Carolina. ... I was amazed at the joy in the city. ...

There was, in Philadelphia's State House steeple, a gigantic bell weighing 2,080 pounds. People rang this bell on important occasions. It rang when George III was made king. It was muffled and tolled when a ship sailed up the Delaware bearing the hated stamps. The bell rang to bring the people to the State House to hear the trouble about tea and to hear resolutions concerning it. The bell tolled when the news arrived that the British had closed the port of Boston. It summoned the people of Philadelphia to hear about Lexington and Concord. The bell may not have pealed that night, but eventually it rang in the cause of Liberty.

Copies of the Declaration were printed by the thousands. Express riders galloped out of the city with copies of the very important document in their dispatch cases.

The Declaration was a big step forward, but people could see it was extremely important that the colonies be united. On June 12, 1776, a committee headed by John Dickinson, patriot from Maryland and Pennsylvania, presented to Congress "The Articles of Confederation and Perpetual Union."

The Articles gave Congress certain powers over war, peace,

money, the postal system and other things, and provided for one vote for each state. But the states first had to ratify, or approve, the Articles before they would take effect. And before the Articles were ratified (it took almost five years), many people suffered wounds, death, or disease from the war, and much work had to be done.

However, people were disappointed in the Articles, for they did not make for a strong United States.[1] Much work faced Congress and the patriots.

[1] Because the Articles did not form a strong government, they led to the Constitutional Convention of 1787, which drafted the Constitution of the United States.

Chapter 9

SERGEANT JASPER DISPLAYS THE SPIRIT
OF SOUTH CAROLINA

FIVE months before the Declaration of Independence, a leader
in South Carolina wanted the colonies to break from England.
This man was Christopher Gadsden, a delegate to Congress. But
other congressmen did not think the time ripe for such an idea—
it seemed too radical.

South Carolina contained many Tories, but most of its citizens were patriots who were unhappy with the Crown. They
disliked the British custom of refusing to give Americans jobs in
governing the colony. When the hated blue stamps required by
the Stamp Act arrived eleven years before the Declaration,
Charleston refused to let the stamps be brought ashore. When
the argument over tea arose, not one pound of it was sold in
South Carolina.

In late 1775, the patriots were furious. They discovered
that agents of the King were stirring up the Indians. The British
idea was to get the Cherokees on the warpath, thinking this would
drive the patriots into accepting the King's form of government,
or that it would serve as punishment. Chief Dragging Canoe of
the Cherokees soon had the border in dread of the torch and the
tomahawk.[1]

[1] This border warfare took place in what is now Georgia and Tennessee.

Suddenly, in early 1776, came a ghastly message from George Washington. He warned that South Carolina might be invaded. A letter telling of the British plans had been intercepted. The trouble was the letter did not say exactly what part of the Southern coast would be struck.

On the British side, the facts were that the former governor of South Carolina, Lord William Campbell, assured General Clinton in New York that the job of taking South Carolina would be simple. The former governor said that the Tories would rise and attack. Lord Campbell also told the general that he himself would come along.

When George Washington's message of warning arrived in Charleston, South Carolina, the defense work speeded up. To help the South Carolinians, General Washington sent General Charles Lee to the colony. Lee was said to be a great leader, skilled in war. He ranked high on the list of American generals.

When Lee arrived, he looked at the fort the patriots were building on Sullivans Island and made fun of it. Lee, who was both opinionated and rude, called the fort "nothing but a death-trap—a mere slaughter pen."

The patriots were stung. It seemed to them that the fort, which was a double square pen made of palmetto logs bolted to-gether, would stand a hard beating. The space between the two walls was filled with sand. The biggest trouble in the patriots' eyes was that the fort was not finished on two sides.

Soon after Lee arrived, an express rider rode into town. He had exciting news. The British fleet was twenty miles away. The people feared that their city might be reduced to ashes. Fathers made hurried arrangements to have their families taken to the country. John Rutledge, who had been chosen as governor of the colony, called out the militia. At the fort, the work went ahead with a rush. General Lee shook his head with disgust. He

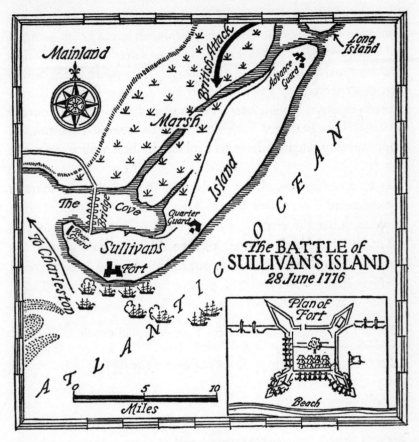

MAP NO. 6

pointed out that the fort had but sixty-two guns; there were fifty vessels in sight.

But Rutledge and his principal military man, the pleasant Colonel William Moultrie, refused to scare. To them, the fort had great value.[2] General Lee said that, if men were to stay in the "deathtrap" and face the British warships, at least another

---

[2] This fort was later named Fort Moultrie in honor of its commander.

avenue of escape (another bridge) should be built in a hurry. Rutledge and Moultrie disregarded this advice.

When Sir Henry Clinton's army appeared off Charleston, packed aboard eight men-of-war, there was a panic in the town. People expected the fight to begin any minute. But the British were in no rush. Twenty-seven days went by. It was hot; clouds of mosquitoes bothered both sides. The enemy used the time to send scouting parties ashore to explore the best way to take the town.

It became obvious, after a while, that the British would attack the palmetto fort. After it was battered into submission, they could conquer the city.

General Lee made another plea to Rutledge to abandon the fort. Governor Rutledge wrote out his answer and had it carried to the fort:

Colonel Moultrie,
Genl. Lee wishes to evacuate the Fort. You will not do so without an order from me.
I will cut off my right hand sooner than write it.

JOHN RUTLEDGE

When the British were ready, they sent a flag of truce ashore with an officer. But the Americans fired on the flag and the officer returned to the fleet. This embarrassed Rutledge and he apologized. The next day the British did this again. This time the officer under the white flag was received courteously. He delivered a lecture from Sir Henry Clinton on how terrible a civil war was, and the message that if the patriots would surrender at once there would be a free pardon for all.

Rutledge and his followers were not the type to listen to this kind of talk.

The warships drew up in a double line near the fort. They had

287 guns aiming at it. The battle began—the fort against eight war vessels. The guns of the fort were fixed; not all of them could fire at the ships. The men-of-war took careful aim. The *boom* of the guns brought out the town's citizens to places where they could see the battle. Clouds of black powder shrouded the fort and the ships.

The question of powder supply hung over the officers in Fort Sullivan like a dagger. General Lee was rowed to the fort through the British fire. He pointed a gun or two at the enemy vessels, then advised, "If your powder gives out, spike your guns and retreat."

A force of Redcoats landed on Long Island and tried to cross the inlet. The patriots were ready for that and they sent Colonel Thompson to oppose them with infantrymen, cannoneers, and grapeshot. The Redcoat landing party was handicapped, not only by Colonel Thompson's force, but by high water in the inlet. They could not get across. Then Lee left for Charleston.

Three British warships tried to sail into the cove in rear of the fort but got stuck in the mud.

The cable holding the flagship, *Bristol*, fast to its anchor was cut, and the ship swung so that its prow faced the fort. The guns from the fort raked it fore and aft. The ship was almost torn to pieces. Many men were wounded, including the admiral, Sir Peter Parker, who had his pants blown off. The captain of the *Bristol* was killed.

In the thick of the fight, the blue flag of South Carolina, which had a white crescent in the upper corner near the pole, was shot away from its staff.

Sergeant William Jasper left his gun crew and sprang up on the parapet. He ran the length of the embankment and jumped down to get the flag. The cannon balls from the ships thudded into the spongy palmetto logs near his head. He grabbed the flag

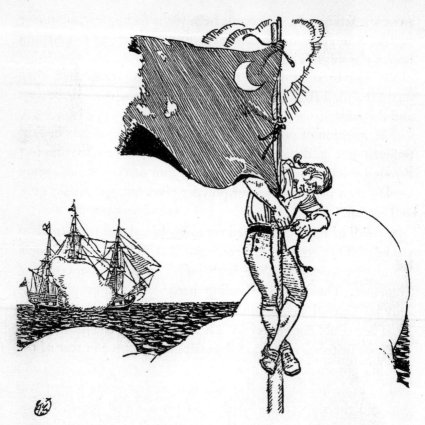

and got safely back into the fort. He gave three cheers after he fixed the flag to a ramrod and placed it back in position.

Finally, the British stopped the fighting and the warships withdrew down the bay. In accordance with the gallant customs of the day, General Lee sent fresh fruit aboard the flagship for General Clinton with his compliments. The Britisher sent back beer and cheese.

The patriots were wild with happiness when they saw the ships pull away. Governor Rutledge visited Fort Sullivan and thanked the men. He singled out Sergeant Jasper and gave him his sword, offering him a commission as an officer. William Jasper accepted the sword with thanks, but he refused the commission because he could neither read nor write.

For hundreds of years men have revered their flags. The separate colonies had flags of their own. The flag of Massachusetts bore a pine tree, New York had a white flag with a black beaver. (The idea of the New York flag was to show that the people were industrious. It was also a salute to the fur trade.) Rhode Island used a blue flag with a white anchor and the word "HOPE." All over the colonies men soon heard how the brave Sergeant Jasper had shown the spirit of the colony's patriots by rescuing the flag of South Carolina.

When news of the battle reached England, the people could hardly believe it. The word that a British fleet, commanded by a British admiral, had been unable to capture a palmetto-log fort sitting on a sandbank and firing only sixty-two guns sounded too strange to be true. This battle encouraged the people of South Carolina who believed in the Revolution.

The patriots of the colony turned on the Cherokees and defeated them.

The Tories were agonized by the British failure, but they were far from convinced that the patriots would win out in the end. The Tories looked forward to the return of the Redcoats, but they would have a long two-year wait.

Chapter 10

DESPERATE DAYS IN NEW YORK AND
NEW JERSEY

ALTHOUGH George Washington and the American Army were fortifying New York City and Long Island in the summer of 1776, the Tories were certain that their side would eventually win. They were encouraged by William Tryon, the former governor of New York, who had no love for the patriots. Tryon was in the harbor, safe aboard the British man-of-war, *Dutchess of Gordon*. He sent word ashore to the Tories (and it leaked to Washington's army) that General Howe would arrive shortly with his army on board a tremendous fleet. The Tories felt that all they had to do was to weather the storm.

The Tories became bolder. Some did their best to weaken the money system of the colonies by distributing counterfeit paper money; others acted as spies, sending word to Tryon of the locations where General Washington was placing men and cannon. The patriots reacted. In nearby Connecticut, they caught a parson of Loyalist sympathies who was laden with false money, and made him eat some. In New York City, certain Tories had their clothes removed, were daubed with hot tar, and ridden about the streets on sharp rails. The excitement reached a peak when it was discovered there was on foot a Tory plot to murder

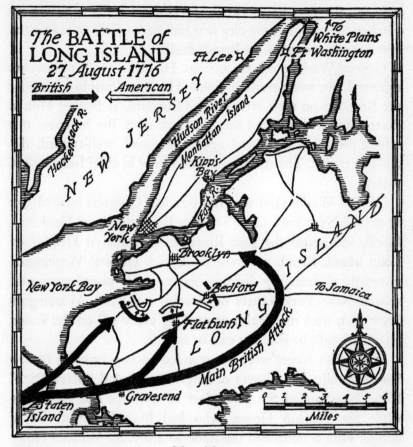

MAP No. 7

George Washington.[1] The patriots moved rapidly. The ring-leaders in the plot, who included the mayor of New York, were imprisoned. Private Thomas Hickey, of Washington's own guard, was found guilty and hanged.

The spirits of the Loyalists soared when patriotic lookouts,

---

[1] The scheme was said to have been originated by Governor Tryon who, it was alleged, furnished money to bribe the men in the plot.

enjoying the June breezes at Sandy Hook, far down New York Harbor, sent word to the city that hundreds of sail were in sight. It was the vanguard of the British fleet.

General Washington was anxious. His army numbered twenty thousand, but was it ready to fight? The Americans had punished the Redcoats on their retreat from Concord, at Bunker Hill, at Boston, and had repulsed them at Charleston. But he knew that a long campaign lay ahead against seasoned, well-trained, disciplined troops. The American commander in chief had cause to worry.

General Washington was also puzzled. Congress insisted that he defend New York City. The city lay at the tip of Manhattan Island, and across the East River stood Brooklyn Heights on Long Island. Islands are hard to defend. General Washington solved the situation by dividing his army. He placed some men around New York, others on Brooklyn Heights. Washington knew that, with the British controlling every sail on the water, his army might be sliced in two or cut off.

The British forces were commanded by two brothers from a famous family—the Howes of England. Admiral "Black Dick" Howe commanded the great fleet of warships and transports, while Sir William Howe, who had braved patriot fire at Bunker Hill, commanded the Redcoat army. Sir William Howe was a skillful leader—although he was usually ready to put aside the work of leadership in favor of a good time. And Sir William was not entirely sympathetic with the manner in which the King was governing the colonies or the idea of war. Nevertheless, he had his duty to do.

It was at this time that copies of the Declaration of Independence arrived in New York City. General Washington had the important paper read to the troops at evening parade. There were loud cheers by the soldiers. A mob, to the general's disgust,

threw a rope on the statue of King George III and tugged it down. The lead in the statue was soon on its way to Litchfield, Connecticut, where ladies of the town made it into bullets. The Tories were sure the patriots were crazy.

The day after the statue was torn down, the British landed on Staten Island. The enemy army totaled twelve thousand more than Washington's army, and it was backed by a powerful fleet which covered much of the harbor. To the Tories, the British Army and Navy were an answer to the Declaration of Independence.

But the British had their troubles, too. They were fighting far from home, and this meant a long supply line. It took from two to four months, depending upon the winds at sea, for guns, ammunition, food, and other supplies to reach them. And, because their army was small, the British hired German soldiers from the various petty principalities. For instance, the British paid the Prince of Hesse thirty-five dollars for each soldier killed, twelve dollars for each one wounded, and five hundred thousand dollars per year for the loan of ten thousand of his Hessians. While the German officers would fight alongside the Redcoats, the difference in language and the difficulties in getting along, which allies always have, made things harder than if these ten thousand soldiers had been Englishmen.

And the German soldiers needed time to get in shape to fight. They had received bad food on the long trip across the Atlantic and their living quarters aboard ship were so cramped they had to sleep on the deck and in the hold "spoon fashion"—that is, in rows, all facing the same way. The only manner in which they could turn over was for the entire row to turn at the same time. They did this, when they were ready to shift position, by having a noncommissioned officer shout, "*About, face!*"

On the American side, sight of the enemy caused the work of improving defenses to move faster, and the positions improved.

The Howe brothers first tried to treat with the Americans in an effort to stop the war. Black Dick sent a letter by a messenger under a white flag into the American lines to General Washington, but the letter was addressed to "George Washington, Esq. &c. &c."

George Washington's adjutant refused to receive the letter. The general explained to American friends that he was not acting stuffily, but that he was a general and he was determined that Lord Howe undervalue neither him nor the Continental Army.[2]

Late in August, 1776, the British landed troops on Long Island near Gravesend, eight miles south of Brooklyn. The impressive fighter, General Cornwallis, was there. So was General Clinton. And so was the famous Black Watch Regiment, tough High-landers, garbed in dark plaid kilts. The drums rumbled as the Germans came ashore in their gaudy uniforms. The Hessians wore white breeches and blue coats, high, tapering helmets of shiny brass, crowned with woolen pompons. Others, the Jaegers, wore large cocked black hats with a splash of red about the collars of their green uniforms.

General Washington made a last-minute change in his Long Island force before the fight by putting Israel Putnam in place of Major General Nathanael Greene, who was ill with malaria. There was no braver man in the army than Old Put, but he was not familiar with the ground on Long Island. This was a hard turn of events for the patriots because General Nat Greene was one of Washington's cleverest generals.

The British began to move just about dark. They swung around toward Jamaica and had the good fortune to capture a patrol of five American officers who were asleep. These officers had been furnished horses so they could send in messages rapidly to General Putnam if the British came their way, but they failed to stay alert. As a result, the British closed in fast from the flank. This was a complete surprise. To move cannon quietly, the British used saws instead of axes, when trees had to be cut, so as not to let the Americans hear them coming. And at the same time the British made a hot attack on the American center.

The Continental Army on Long Island was now in a bad fix.

---

[2] There is no doubt but that this slight by Lord Howe was entirely unintentional; he and his brother wanted to make peace and to have things back where they were before trouble started.

They were in their trenches on Brooklyn Heights and were cut off by the East River.

Even though the British fleet was near at hand, General Washington sent for all the boats that could be found on the river, and he persuaded some of his troops to go back and face the enemy. When night arrived, Washington hurriedly placed men on scows, rafts, barges, sailboats, skiffs, canoes—anything that would float—and the army escaped to Manhattan. The secret movement was helped by a wind which kept Black Dick from landing more troops, and then by a heavy fog. When a Tory woman discovered the Americans were leaving, she sent a Negro to inform the British. Luckily for the Americans, the Negro ran into a Hessian who did not understand him and placed him under arrest!

The American Army was saved from destruction by its eye-teeth but it was now on another island, and the British still commanded the water. There was danger that the British might land farther north on Manhattan Island and capture Washington and his whole army.

General Washington divided his forces between Manhattan and Kingsbridge. Great pressure was on him; things looked black.

There was talk of burning the town so the British could not use it. John Jay, a wealthy patriot and landowner in New York City, had not been in favor of the colonies leaving the Crown, but now, after the Declaration, he was doing his best to help the cause. He urged Washington to burn the city, but orders arrived from Congress for Washington to spare it.

Now the British warships and transports sailed up the East River and landed at Kip's Bay. The Continentals in lower Manhattan were cut off, and as soon as they could they ran for the rear. Fire broke out in New York City and over four hundred homes were burned.

In a well-organized withdrawal, the soldiers protect each other. Units are assigned to help other units get to the rear. Ground is given up slowly; the enemy receives plenty of fire; there is no panic. But in this retreat there was no order. The troops were excited. It was every man for himself. The Americans abandoned guns, cannons, tools, food, baggage, and tents. George Washington tried to stop his men from running but he could not. He had never been so angry. He threw his hat on the ground and shouted, "Are these the men with which I am to defend America?" His pleadings did no good, for the soldiers were crazy with fear. When a brigadier general ran out of the bushes and streaked for the rear with his men, Washington caught the general, stopped him, and whipped him with his cane. Other officers ran. General Washington was furious.

General Howe could have pursued the fleeing patriots, but he accomplished what he had planned. He started to fortify New York City. Maybe Washington would attack. But Washington had no idea of attacking. He set down his reasons and the exasperating situation in a letter to Congress:

... On our side, the war should be defensive.... We are now in a [dangerous] position. Declining an engagement to fight may throw discouragement over the minds of many, but when the fate of America may be at stake, we should continue the war as long as possible. ...

George Washington was telling Congress the only way in which the small Continental Army could exist was *to fight defensively, to attack only when victory was certain.*

This was a hard decision to make, for it is the offensive that usually wins. But two things happened which showed the spirit of the fighting Americans. Over on Long Island, a young man named Nathan Hale of Connecticut, a graduate of Yale University, had been captured. Lieutenant Hale, of the Continental

Army, had volunteered for hazardous duty as a spy, and had been assigned to discover the British plans. Hale gave the impression to the Long Islanders and the British that he was a teamster, and he made notes about the British and Germans. The enemy recognized him as a spy and did not even give him a trial. He was treated brutally. He was not allowed to have a clergyman, and his last letters home were destroyed. They hustled Hale to the scaffold. When the noose was placed about his neck, Nathan Hale spoke. *"I only regret,"* he said, *"that I have but one life to lose for my country."*

At Harlem Heights, Thomas Knowlton, a popular lieutenant colonel of Virginia riflemen, reported to George Washington. "I sent for you," said the commander in chief, "because I want information of the British plans. I want to lay a trap for them." He sent Thomas Knowlton and one hundred and twenty volunteers, most of them from Connecticut, on a circular movement, deep into the country which probably would soon be occupied by the enemy. Knowlton's Rangers had to retreat after a hot battle. Knowlton himself was killed. The British sounded their bugles to insult the Americans, as if to say, "This is nothing but a fox chase."

Now a real fight developed, and many of the Americans who streaked for the rear at Kip's Bay fought better. But this was not the place where Washington thought it safe to bring on a big battle.

The British now tried to trap the Americans by landing in their rear at Pell's Point. This made General Washington move his army to White Plains, except for the men inside Fort Washington and Fort Lee.

At Fort Washington were some of the best troops in the army—three thousand of them—men from Pennsylvania, Maryland, and Virginia. On the day before the battle, the British sent an officer under protection of a white flag to Fort Washington.

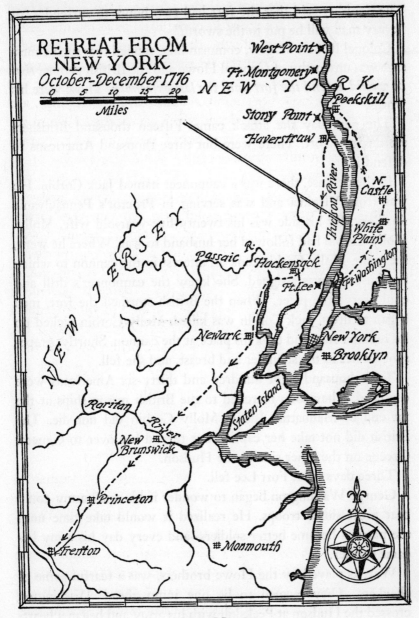

MAP No. 8

The Britisher said that the fort had two hours to surrender, or "every man will be put to the sword."

Colonel Robert Magaw, commanding, replied that such a message was unworthy of General Howe and the British people; *that he would defend the fort until the last extremity.* Those were his words.

The next day the attack came. Fifteen thousand Britishers stormed the fort. There were but three thousand Americans to defend it.

In the defense, there was a cannoneer named Jack Corbin. He was from Virginia and was serving in Proctor's Pennsylvania Artillery. By his side was his twenty-five-year-old wife, Molly. Molly Corbin had followed her husband to war. Where he went, she went. Molly Corbin took an interest in the cannon to which her husband was assigned. She knew the cannoneer's drill and could serve the piece. When the British stormed the fort, men began to drop. Jack Corbin was killed. Molly Corbin picked up his rammer staff and took his place at the cannon. Shortly, grapeshot hit her in the shoulder and breast, and she fell.

Two thousand eight hundred and thirty-six Americans were captured. They soon marched to the British prison ships at the far end of Manhattan Island. Molly Corbin did not die. The British did not take her captive but turned her over to General Greene on the other side of the Hudson.

Three days later, Fort Lee fell.

George Washington began to wonder if his small army could beat professional troops. He realized it would take time until the patriots became better soldiers—and every day his army became smaller.

War, as played by the Howe brothers, was a fearful game of checkers. They seemed to be one jump ahead. Washington crossed the Hudson at Peekskill with his army and began a heartbreaking retreat across New Jersey. Right behind him in close pursuit marched Cornwallis.

On the retreat, the patriots struggled to keep up. To fall behind meant capture or death. The withdrawal across the flatlands of New Jersey became a rout. At one place where the two armies clashed, two "brigades" of Washington's men ran away and left him within eighty yards of the enemy. Had Washington been captured, or killed, in all probability the Revolution would have ended shortly.

Now the general sent an urgent message to General Charles Lee, who had over seventy-five hundred of his best soldiers at White Plains, to come at once. If ever a commander in chief was in trouble, it was George Washington.

But Lee did not desire to obey Washington's orders! He did not move.

The November weather was cold and rainy; the spirits of Washington's men sank lower and lower as they marched ahead. Now Washington received an outrageous blow: he discovered by opening mail addressed to his adjutant that General Charles Lee not only did not wish to march to Jersey, but that Lee was critical of him. And, further, Washington discovered that one of his best friends, his adjutant, Colonel Joseph Reed, was also critical of him. Colonel Reed and Washington parted company. These were two hard blows; but Washington marched on, determined not to despair or to give up.

The weather became colder; the muddy roads froze. Everything hinged on General Lee's joining Washington—and rapidly. But Lee still delayed. Washington wrote him several times, and received answers from Lee saying he did not know if it were best to attack the enemy in the rear or to join Washington. Washington replied patiently—for he felt Lee was his best general. Had the situation been better, Washington would have been happy to have Lee strike the enemy from behind, but Lee was needed badly to reinforce the fast-dwindling army. It was a critical time.

But Lee not only delayed joining General Washington, he wrote one of his generals, Horatio Gates, that "a certain great man is damnably deficient." Of course, he meant George Washington.

Hardly had Lee signed his faithless and disloyal letter when a British cavalry patrol walked into a tavern where Lee was staying. The experienced and egotistical General Lee had failed to post a guard even though he was far from his army, and the British troopers rode off with their famous prisoner garbed in a dressing gown.

Washington did not know of the capture when he reached the banks of the Delaware. He did not delay, but placed his men in boats and retreated across the river. Then Washington had every boat for miles up and down the river taken away so Lord Cornwallis could not get them.

When the British general arrived at the river, he was determined to get across somehow, but General Howe called a halt. He said, "We will winter in Trenton and fight in the spring."

A mounted messenger, covered with mud and dirt, rode up to George Washington a few days later and handed him an express from Major General John Sullivan telling Lee had been captured. In reality, the enemy had done the Continental Army a favor.

Shortly, General Sullivan arrived with Lee's men, and General Gates came in with more. Washington had some men again, but he was worried because many enlistments expired at the end of the year, which was only a few days away.

In the meantime, up on Lake Champlain in the summer of 1776, a strange "sea" fight was shaping up. One of the best young generals in the British Army, the dashing Sir Guy Carleton, was putting together three large ships and ten gunboats at St. Johns.[3] These warships had been taken apart so they could be hauled overland and around the falls in the Richelieu River. Other ships were pulled through the dangerous rapids. When Sir Guy was finally ready to move, he had a fleet of twenty-nine ships of war and over four hundred bateaux. He placed on them his army of about thirteen thousand—a mixture of British, Canadians, Hessians, and Indians—and set sail up the lake. He hoped to capture the fortress at Ticonderoga and then push on to New York and join forces with General Howe.

The only thing in his way was a fighter, Benedict Arnold, and numbers of fellow Americans from Connecticut, Maine, and Massachusetts. These men worked feverishly to build warships out of green lumber while Benedict Arnold, still suffering from the wound he received at Quebec, limped about taking care of their needs and encouraging them. Arnold's "navy" caught his aggressive spirit, although only a handful had ever seen war on water.

When Carleton's force sailed up the lake, Arnold's crazy-looking fleet surprised them sixty miles north of Fort Ti. In a day-long cannonade, the Americans were beaten, but they kept General Carleton's armada from heading farther south.

During the night, Arnold's battered ships limped away to Crown Point, not far from Fort Ti. He and his men burned their boats so Carleton could not capture them. Then Arnold got ready to fight on shore.

But Carleton decided that winter was too close for him to undertake a campaign, so he wisely withdrew to Canada.

The determined fight of Benedict Arnold was a tremendous help to the war effort of the Americans. If Carleton had gotten through, the situation would have been so one-sided Washington

[3] See Map No. 3, page 28.

and his men could not have existed as an army, and the patriots might have lost heart.

As it was, George Washington was greatly outnumbered when he escaped across the Delaware.

In the Tory center of New York, the Loyalists worked to repair the burned part of the town. They were unworried about General Carleton's failure to get through on the invasion route; they were confident he would make it in the spring. The Tories were happy. New York City was their refuge, and Washington and his ragged army had been chased across the Delaware. Surely the Revolution was on its last legs.

Chapter 11

THE SPIRIT OF 1776

T HE American cause was at low ebb. The patriots were downcast over the retreat through New Jersey and the capture of General Charles Lee. Around this soldier of fortune, who had refused to obey Washington's orders, was an odor of treason, but few suspected Lee. To almost everyone, his capture seemed to be another calamity. And when word leaked through the lines that the British were treating General Lee as a deserter from their army instead of a prisoner of war, the patriots became excited. Washington acted, for he was not suspicious of Lee. The commander in chief sent a message to the enemy, asking that General Lee be exchanged and allowed to join the American Army, but the British were in no hurry to carry out the request.

The icy winds and snow made the land as bleak as the American hopes. Washington feared his army would become even smaller because many enlistments of the soldiers would soon expire. It was a time of crisis. Tom Paine, the best-known writer in America, used the word, *Crisis*, not only to sum up the situation but as a title for a pamphlet. He wrote:

These are the times that try men's souls. . . . The summer soldier and the sunshine patriot will, in this crisis, shrink from the service

of their country....I love the man that can smile in trouble....He
whose heart is firm will pursue his principles unto death....

Once again Paine's words aroused courage in the men who
were carrying the burden of the Revolution—not only at the
front but at home.

Congress now acted in response to the pleas of an unusual
soldier who refused to acknowledge defeat—General Washington. Congress awarded a bounty of twenty dollars, one hundred
acres of land, and a suit of clothes for each man who enlisted
for the duration of the war; then it weakened this offer by saying
that a man could enlist for three years.[1] There was not a great
response, but when the German soldiers began looting and other
outrageous actions against the patriot families in New Jersey, men
began to report to the American Army for duty.

Congress now made a smart move; it sent a secret commission
to France, headed by Ben Franklin, to try to get help. Franklin
sailed on the sloop, *Reprisal,* taking along his two young grand-
sons. The voyage was dangerous. If the British Navy had captured the *Reprisal,* Franklin would have dangled at the end of a
rope, and the two boys would have become captives. But instead
of being captured, the *Reprisal* took two British merchantmen as
prizes of war and landed Franklin and his party on the coast of
France.

Ben Franklin created excitement in Paris. Crowds watched Ben
when he appeared on the streets. Men wore "Franklin" hats. Old
Ben Franklin had never been more popular.

But the British spies found out quickly that Franklin was in
France and what he was trying to accomplish. The British ambassador, Stormont, protested to the French King. He said that
the courtesies and attention Ben Franklin, Silas Deane, and
Arthur Lee (the other two members of the commission) were

---

[1] This was December, 1776. The war lasted until October, 1781.

receiving were most unfriendly to Great Britain. But the King of France did nothing; the French people loved Ben Franklin's cheerfulness and his wit. For instance, when Viscount Stormont published a report saying that George Washington had lost four thousand men in a single fight, Ben said that the truth was one thing and Stormont another. The French laughed over this, and in slang made the name "Stormont" stand for "one who does not tell the truth."

Ben Franklin's mission was successful in obtaining a secret loan of four hundred thousand dollars from France. This was a tremendous help because Congress had no way to tax the people; the only way it could support the American Army was by securing loans. It was not long before a new type of flintlock musket, better than the Brown Bess, appeared in the American Army as a result of this loan.

Washington also pledged his own money to help the army, and so did Colonel John Stark of New Hampshire and other officers. Part of the money went to pay spies, although the spies were not anxious to go into the towns occupied by the enemy. The spies were afraid they would be recognized by Tories and hanged.

Everyone knew the British had scattered troops over a large area in New Jersey: from Perth Amboy in the Lower Bay, south of Newark, to Mount Holly, east of Philadelphia. But this was not detailed enough information for General Washington. However, one spy, a brave man named John Honeywell, who lived in Trenton, played a trick. He allowed himself to be "captured" by American scouts and brought before Washington. Honeywell told the commander in chief the troops in Trenton were Hessians under Colonel Rall, who was extremely careless. The spy also gave information about the locations of the enemy in Trenton.

George Washington determined to strike. He chose Christmas Day for the move, because he knew that the Hessian custom on

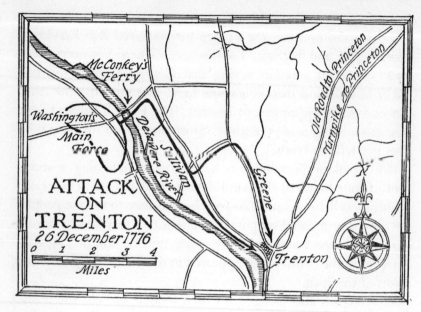

MAP No. 9

Christmas called for day-long feasting and drinking; there would probably be no patrolling or scouting by the Hessians. Washington believed he could win.

The fearless American leader took two thousand four hundred men and eighteen pieces of artillery, and marched them to a place opposite McConkey's Ferry.[2] He sent other forces south along the river to cross near Assunpink Creek, in the hope of cutting off the Hessian retreat if the attack were successful.

The Delaware was choked with ice and, in the fading light at six in the evening, it did not look favorable for a small-boat crossing. But the boats were at the riverbank and Washington gave the go-ahead order. The boats were sturdy but narrow; they were used in peacetime to haul iron ore. The loading and

[2] See Map No. 8, page 85.

transporting of the artillery and the horses that pulled the guns was dangerous; but on duty to supervise the job was Henry Knox, who had had experience before with cannon under risky circumstances.

Washington made the dangerous crossing with his small army, and once on the other side he sent his men to Trenton in two columns. It was 3 A.M. when the last cannon was placed on the icy bank. The crossing had taken nine hard hours.

It began to snow and sleet. The roads became so slippery both men and animals had trouble standing up. It was dark and cold. Ahead lay nine icy miles. The soldiers were not clothed or shod properly for winter. Some men were shoeless and left a trail of blood in the snow.

In Trenton, the enemy was not alert. Colonel Rall was at the home of Abraham Hunt, drinking wine and playing cards. A man rushed in and gave him a written message. It was from a Tory, telling him of the secret march on Trenton, but Rall had no time to look at messages and shoved the paper into his pocket.

When Washington's two columns arrived and set up their artillery, the Hessian regiment on guard discovered them. It was eight o'clock on the morning of December 26.

The Hessian drummers beat *"Call to Arms."* The European soldiers ran out of the houses to be greeted by grapeshot and cannon balls. Colonel Rall ran out. The Hessians were confused. Street fighting began. Americans seemed to be everywhere. Colonel Rall tried to get his men to charge, and he himself fell mortally wounded. The Americans used their bayonets.

The confusion, the yelling of the Americans, and their cannon fire and bayonet work were too much. Some Hessians escaped, but over one thousand became prisoners of war and were immediately sent back over the river to Philadelphia. Thirty Hessians were killed; the Americans lost four (two frozen to death and two wounded). General Washington made a call on Colonel

Rall, who had been carried into a house and was dying. In Rall's pocket was the message he had been too busy to read.

General Howe was shocked by the news of Washington's surprise victory. General Cornwallis rushed troops to the scene and took position along Assunpink Creek and, because the Americans were in Trenton, Cornwallis confidently assured his British Regulars, "At last we have run down the old fox. We'll bag him in the morning."

But the "fox" refused to stand still. Washington detailed a

few men to keep the campfires burning all night and several others to make as much noise as they could by digging. The British sentries did not worry—they thought they could see and hear their enemy. But when morning came, the "fox" and his army were well on their way to Princeton. The British worried. They had a big supply depot at New Brunswick, north of Princeton.

Washington's men were exhausted, but there was no time for rest; to stop meant death or capture. They pushed on through rain and then over frozen roads to Princeton. Here they crashed into three regiments of British Regulars.

A hot fight developed. Washington galloped up astride a huge white horse to see for himself. He was fearless; he rode within thirty yards of the enemy line. So inspired were his men, they outfought the British. The Americans looked like scarecrows when they entered Princeton, but they were victors.

Now Washington marched northwest to Morristown, New Jersey, where he took up a strong position. His men found shelter in villages near Morristown and also built log huts.

The effects of Washington's strike across the Delaware gave high hopes to the dying American cause. British generals began to fear him. People of all types, Tories, British, Hessians, patriots, and neutrals, realized that George Washington had become a fine general and an inspiring battle leader.

The attack on Trenton was the most critical time in George Washington's career. It was a turning point in the Revolutionary War. Had it failed, the American cause would have been in great danger.

When news of the Delaware crossing and the two victories reached France, there was enthusiasm among the French people. Ben Franklin was besieged by officers of all ranks who wanted him to recommend them to General Washington so they could take their place in the Continental Army. Franklin finally drew up a paper which he said was a model letter of recommendation. It said:

The bearer of this, who is going to America, presses me to give him a letter of recommendation, though I know nothing of him, not even his name [and] as to his character and merits, I must refer you to himself. . . .

But a wealthy nineteen-year-old Frenchman, the Marquis de Lafayette, did not bother Ben Franklin. When young Lafayette heard the news, he outfitted a ship at his own expense and loaded it with supplies furnished by another Frenchman who admired the Americans, Pierre Beaumarchais. The King of France ordered Lafayette not to sail, for he feared the ship would cause trouble for France, but Lafayette put to sea. When he arrived in South Carolina, he hired wagons and buggies to carry the uniforms and equipment and supplies overland nine hundred miles to Philadelphia. Congress rewarded him with the commission of a major general. George Washington was not favorably impressed with the idea of a foreigner receiving such high rank in the Continental Army, but when he met the young Frenchman he liked him, and they became friends.

But hard cash was needed at once to pay the army and to buy food. George Washington wrote a banker in Philadelphia, one of the signers of the Declaration, Robert Morris. The general made a strong plea and Robert Morris did not fail. He gave all he could of his own fortune and went from house to house to obtain the rest. He raised fifty thousand dollars in this manner and sent it to the general.

For six months the front was quiet.

The patriot army had nearly been demolished, but its great leader, Washington, had infused the men who had stuck by him with the Spirit of 1776. With such a leader, the little American Army had become a force to be respected. With all its troubles, it would fight on—it would not quit. But hard days lay ahead.

Chapter 12

START OF THE YEAR OF
"THE BLOODY 7'S"

In the cold January of 1777 at Morristown, Washington's army began to melt away and it looked as if the patriot cause were failing.

Trenton had been an important victory, but Washington's little army was in bad shape. Few responded to pleas to enlist. Washington pounded Congress. He said the lackadaisical attitude of many patriots was unbelievable. There was little food, the medical department was pitiful, the equipment poor; there were few blankets, little clothing, and men were not paid on time.

Word spread of the horrible treatment of captured Americans on British prison ships and this hindered enlistment. Further, all knew in the spring Washington's army would face once again professional soldiers from Europe. Under such circumstances, and with no traditions to bind the men of the units together, and with a poor state of discipline existing, the spirit was low in the American Army.

Smallpox and other sickness broke out. If General Howe had attacked Washington's army at Morristown, the result might have been disastrous for the patriots, but fortunately the British general did not believe in winter campaigns.

Congress now tried to help its army by asking people to turn in the names of anyone who deserted, so deserters could be arrested; and Washington said all deserters who returned to their units would be pardoned. But this had little effect. Then the general sent an order to one of his senior officers to "sweep every town from Boston to Peekskill and send in the loiterers." In spite of these actions, the army remained small as long as the weather was cold.

Up in the West Point area on the Hudson River, old General Putnam's clerk, Sergeant Ware, an original speller, wrote General Putnam's thoughts in the orderly book:

More than a Sentury & half ago our fore fathers fled from the Island of Great Britan Crosted the atlantick to avoid the Cruel Persecution & oppression of unrelenting British Tereny and Sought an assilleam a Place of Security than a habitation of wild Beasts and Savages. . . . [The British made intolerable] Demands upon us from time to time and now at Length have Drawn their Swords and Like Outdatious Robers thretten to take away our Lives. . . . By the Laws of God & man we have the greatest Right to Injoy . . . & Motive is great.

But in spite of thoughts like these from the leaders, the soldiers in Washington's army continued to desert.

The general decided it would help if the thousand Continentals and the militia he had left could be improved. He tightened discipline. When a deserter was caught he was brought before a court-martial, and this often resulted in the soldier being flogged. Sometimes captured deserters were forced to run the gantlet between two long lines of soldiers who were armed with sticks and clubs. When such a man reached the other end of the line, he was usually in no condition to walk. Some deserters were hanged—but men still deserted. The problem of drunkenness also bothered the leader. Drunks received harsh treatment.

Drills began, and for the officers it was etiquette school after drill. Exercise was ordered. The men could see General Wash-

ington keeping himself in shape by riding horseback and playing catch with a ball with other officers. Washington worked hard to improve his army.

Congress added to General Washington's troubles by promoting certain officers to major general and others to brigadier. Quarrels and bickering broke out among senior officers, and the man most upset was Brigadier General Benedict Arnold, for his name had been omitted from the promotion list and five brigadiers were promoted over him. He was furious. Arnold could not understand why he had not been promoted; his bravery, energy, and his skill had been proven. Washington sensed how Arnold would feel and wrote him, "Failure to promote you must have been a mistake. . . . I beg you not to take any hasty steps. . . . I flatter myself I can remedy any error."

However, there were rumors throughout the northern colonies that Arnold's reputation was bad where money was concerned. Some thought him a daring fighter but untrustworthy in money affairs. John Brown, the Massachusetts lawyer who had scouted the Canadians in the dead of winter before the attack on Canada, knew Arnold well. Brown warned, "Money is this man's God, and to get enough of it he would sacrifice his country." But General Washington did not hear Brown's statement, or if he did he did not believe it. Washington could not help Arnold, and Arnold decided to resign from the army.

In April, when General Arnold was getting ready to leave, he rode through western Connecticut and came upon British raiders. The enemy had come ashore from warships under the former governor, Tryon, and had burned a large part of Danbury, destroying five thousand barrels of beef and pork. The Connecticut militia commanded by the elderly general, David Wooster, was trying to stop the raiders. Benedict Arnold reported to Wooster for duty and gave the aged man advice. Arnold found himself commanding Connecticut militia at Ridgefield, and he inspired the men and led them in the attack. The British ran for their ships.

For Arnold's part in the affair, Congress promoted him to major general, but Benedict Arnold remained unhappy—the five generals who were promoted ahead of him still ranked him.

The arguments over who should be promoted were heightened by arrival of foreign officers. At first, these men were thought to be a great help to the American cause, but Washington quickly realized that promotion of foreign officers was unfair to American officers who had proven themselves under fire. In one case, Philippe du Coudrey appeared from France with a letter from

Silas Deane, a member of Ben Franklin's mission. Du Coudrey said Deane had given him a "contract" to be chief of Washington's artillery and ordnance. How Deane could give such a contract was not clear. Washington wrote Congress that if this contract was honored it would be an insult to his great artillery leader, Henry Knox. Du Coudrey "solved" the problem. He fell off a ferry and drowned.

When the snows melted, rumors spread about the British. But no one knew their plan. George Washington would have given much to have discovered it. A sea captain, who had escaped from New York, said the British were getting ready to sail, but he did not know where. Word filtered down from Canada that General John Burgoyne, who had a large army there, would attack Fort Ticonderoga, "the American Gibraltar."

There was some foundation for the rumors which worried Washington, for the British had a three-pronged plan. Of course, it was a closely kept secret and no American knew it.

The plan, which the British thought would win the war, was conceived in an odd way. General Burgoyne had returned to England from Canada. This handsome, young-looking general was a favorite about London. He was well known in the army because of his bravery on the battlefield and for his skill in leading men. The rank and file of the army adored him because he worked to take care of his troops and because he had a cheerful word for everyone. He was popular also because he was a playwright and an amateur actor. In court circles, Gentleman Johnny Burgoyne was a powerful man; he had many friends among both sexes.

One of Burgoyne's friends was Lord George Germain, Secretary of the Colonies. The three-pronged secret plan was the work of both Germain and Burgoyne. It called for three British forces to come in from the north, west, and south and meet at Albany. The makers of the scheme believed that this would cut off New England, then New York would fall, and in turn New England and the southern colonies could be taken when the British chose.

The mechanics of the plan gave one of the largest armies to Gentleman Johnny Burgoyne himself. He would sail down the old invasion route from Canada and capture Fort Ti, annihilating any force of American peasants which came in his way.

A smaller army of British and Tories, reinforced by Mohawk and Iroquois Indians, would be commanded by Lieutenant Colonel Barry St. Leger. This force would sail up the St. Lawrence River into Lake Ontario, land at Oswego, New York, and would smash through the Mohawk Valley, demolishing American forts.

And, sailing up the Hudson, capturing the strong points in the Highlands, would be the army commanded by Sir William Howe. Later, at their leisure, the British would capture Philadelphia, where the Second Continental Congress was meeting. From the British viewpoint, everything looked wonderful.

The King liked this plan and said it was sound. Actually, it was a poor plan. The King did not realize the distances involved. Two of the armies would have to spend much time in wilderness country where there were only crude trails. Not only would travel be difficult, but supplying the two armies would be almost impossible. There could be no co-operation between the three forces, because by the time a messenger traveled the distance to another army the situation would change and, besides, the messenger would be traveling where patriots would be sure to catch him.

To win in war, among other things, the enemy's forces must be defeated. This plan did not have that as an idea. Until George Washington and his men were killed, or until they surrendered, there could be no British victory. *If* Washington's army was defeated, the Revolution would collapse like a punctured balloon.

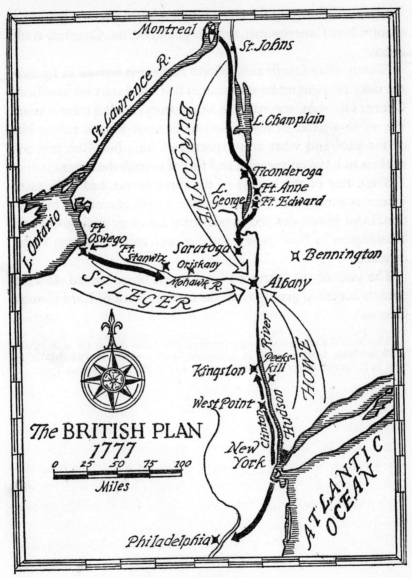

Montreal
St.Johns
St. Lawrence R.
BURGOYNE
L. Champlain
Ticonderoga
L. George
Ft. Anne
Ft. Edward
L. Ontario
Ft. Oswego
Ft. Stanwix
Saratoga
Oriskany
Mohawk R.
Bennington
ST. LEGER
Albany
HOWE
Hudson River
Peeks-kill
Kingston
Clinton
West Point
New York
The BRITISH PLAN
1777
0   25   50   75   100
Miles
Philadelphia
ATLANTIC OCEAN

MAP NO. 10

The idea of attacking the city of Philadelphia, because it was the place where Congress met, was no good because Congress could move.[1]

Shortly after Gentleman Johnny Burgoyne arrived in Canada, the risky plan got under way—and it had a bad start because Lord George Germain, according to an old story, made a terrific error. He wrote a letter of instruction to General Howe, telling him of the plan and what was expected of him, but Germain was anxious to leave on vacation and forgot to mail the letter.

Thus, one of the leaders of the three armies had no idea of what was expected of him or his men. In the absence of instruction, Lord Howe decided to maneuver his army against General Washington in New Jersey and Pennsylvania to capture Philadelphia!

The year of the "three 7's" saw much blood spilled, and the patriots benefited greatly from the careless work of Lord George Germain.

---

[1] The Second Continental Congress moved five times during the war. It was in Philadelphia from 1775-76; in Baltimore from 1776-77; in Philadelphia in 1777; in Lancaster in 1777; in York, 1777-78; and in Philadelphia after 1778.

Chapter 13

BURGOYNE AND ST. LEGER SMASH
TOWARD ALBANY

THE story of Burgoyne's army is one of the most unusual on record.

In the first place, it had almost as many different types of people as a circus. When General Burgoyne was finally ready to take his army into the wilderness, he had: 4,136 British Regulars, 3,116 Germans, 250 Canadians and Tories, 700 wild Indians —a total fighting force of over 8,000. In his artillery train were many bronze cannons and two-wheeled carts to help move the cannon and to carry powder and shot.

Behind this was an enormous wagon train loaded with every type of baggage and supplies from saddles to champagne. Five hundred horses and fifty oxen were on hand to pull the wagons and cannon. In addition, there were hundreds of camp followers, including two hundred wives with their children and servants. Gentleman Johnny Burgoyne had many mouths to feed. Supplies could follow down the two big lakes, Champlain and George; but when the traveling circus pulled away from the lakes, what would happen? General Burgoyne was not worried. He would smash on toward Albany and worry about the supplies later. The thing to do was to beat the enemy.

Along with Burgoyne was the German general, Baron Riedesel, commanding the hired mercenaries. The British Cockneys immediately christened him "Red-hazel." Red-hazel took along his wife, their three young daughters (the youngest was less than a year old), and three servants.

Burgoyne's army was the strangest ever to fight on the North American continent.

A matter of great concern to some of Burgoyne's officers was the seven hundred Indians. Many wondered if they could be controlled. The British general realized the Indians would not be absent when there was fighting—that they would fight on one side or another—and he reasoned they might as well be on the King's side. So General Burgoyne made them a high-sounding speech, which would have put white men to sleep, and hoped all would be well.

The "circus" made a colorful picture as it sailed out of St. Johns in mid-June, 1777, and set a down-lake course for Fort Ticonderoga. The red coats of the British contrasted with the multicolored uniforms of the Germans with their red, yellow, or white facings about the collar and chests. The Indians were stripped to the waist and daubed with war paint. Bands played martial airs when the armada set sail. It was the largest flotilla ever to appear on Lake Champlain. Under sail were twenty-eight gunboats, two hundred flat-bottomed boats, and nine men-of-war of various types. The Indians pulled alongside and paddled far to the front in painted war canoes. When the musicians in the bands rested, fifes and drums entertained the men. It was a gay time—victory looked certain; for the patriots, there could be nothing but defeat.

Fifteen days later, the armada appeared before Fort Ti. Burgoyne called a council of war and upset the German general, Red-hazel, because he did not invite him to take part. (Probably the language difficulty was too great.) As a result of the council, scouts circled the frowning fort on the promontory and began to climb Sugarloaf Mountain,[1] which towered behind the fort.

The American commander inside Fort Ti was General St. Clair. He had only three thousand men—not enough to defend the fort, the ring of mountains behind it, and the heavy wrought-iron chain which was fastened to logs stretching as a barrier across the narrow reach of Lake Champlain.

General St. Clair did not have long to wait before he knew the British plan of attack.

The scouts reported to Gentleman Johnny Burgoyne that Sugarloaf Mountain was unoccupied and Gentleman Johnny agreed with one of his generals, "Where a goat can go, a man can go; and where a man can go, he can drag a gun." He ordered the British to pull two cannons up the steep mountain, and soon General St. Clair saw the fort would be at the mercy of the guns firing down from the mountain. St. Clair felt that it would be slaughter to keep his men in the fort and that he did not have enough to attack the big army down near the lake, so he ordered his patriots to leave. A building took fire in the night while the Americans were withdrawing, and the British saw their enemy retreating. Burgoyne was quick to order a pursuit, and Germans and Indians under Red-hazel defeated the American rear guard.

General Burgoyne felt wonderful. He had seventy miles to go to Albany. The fact that he had only forty days of provisions in his train did not bother him—that could be taken care of later. When news of Burgoyne's victory reached London, King George danced with joy and exclaimed excitedly, "I have beat them! I have beat the Americans!"

The spirits of the patriots in Albany were now at low tide, but they did not give up. When Burgoyne's "circus" rolled southward, overland toward Fort Edward by way of Fort Anne, the

[1] Called Mount Defiance by the British.

patriots had axmen fell trees to block the roads and streams. The march of the British and their allies became slower. Soon they were making less than one mile a day. Supplies were getting lower and lower. Food coming from Canada was delayed. Burgoyne's army was truly floundering in the wilderness.

Progress was so slow General Riedesel had a log cabin built for his wife and children. The baroness was worried about the state of the army (and for the safety of her children), but Burgoyne assured her that "the English never lose ground."

In the meantime, Lieutenant Colonel Barry St. Leger was striking toward Albany from the west in the Mohawk Valley. He had a smaller and faster-moving army than Burgoyne. Traveling with the Britishers under St. Leger were Tories, and a force of Iroquois and Mohawk Indians under the young Mohawk, Joseph Brant.[2] Joseph Brant was a smart and cruel war chief. He and St. Leger were an odd pair. St. Leger, tall and thin, was a battle-hardened officer who had scaled the cliff at Quebec in 1759. The husky Brant wore a feathered headdress, arm bands, and a wide, gaudy sash about his waist. Also with the raiders was the renegade Tory, Colonel John Butler, who had led Indian raids in the past.

It had not been difficult to persuade the Indians to join the expedition to kill patriots. Colonel Guy Johnson, a Britisher, had talked to the Indians at a council meeting and had promised them presents. Johnson said, "Brothers! What can the Americans give you but a piece of bread and a glass of rum? Are you willing to go with them and become their slaves like horses and oxen?" All the Indians needed to take the warpath was a little urging, and in addition the British started paying for American scalps.

Word spread ahead of St. Leger's unholy crew—the patriots

[2] This chief had gone to Eleazar Wheelock's Indian school at Lebanon, Connecticut, and knew how to read and write.

in the beautiful valley knew they had to band together and win to stay alive.

Seven hundred and fifty patriots garrisoned Fort Stanwix.[3] Colonel St. Leger and his men looked the place over and then his cannon began to lob shells into it. Inside, Colonel Peter Gansevoort, a stubborn Mohawk Valley Dutchman, would not surrender. The war whoops of the Indians sounding in the woods about the fort reminded the colonel and his men that if they gave up they would probably face death by torture. And flying from a flagpole of the fort was a flag which inspired them. The banner was made from an old white shirt, a blue jacket captured from the British, and a red cloth from the petticoat of a soldier's wife. It was the first Stars and Stripes to fly over an American fort.[4]

A patriot leader in the valley heard the news of the attack on Fort Stanwix and determined to march to its relief. This leader was a hard-bitten, scrappy fighter, Nicholas Herkimer, "Old Honikol," the patriots called him. General Herkimer rode a white horse that looked as though it had just left the plow. He sent word to the patriot farms that it was once again time to fight for the valley. Patriots answered his call and he led them toward the fort.

But scouts informed Barry St. Leger of General Herkimer's relief column, and St. Leger prepared an ambush for Herkimer in a ravine near Oriskany. It was a clever ambush and well placed.

Old Honikol Herkimer led his men slowly toward the fort. When he neared Stanwix, his common sense told him to be cautious approaching the battle area. He halted. "Scouts join me!"

---

[3] See Map No. 10, page 105.
[4] On June 14, 1777, the Continental Congress passed the following act: "Re- solved—That the flag of the United States be thirteen stripes, alternate red and white; that the union be thirteen stars, white in a blue field, representing a new constellation."
The navy began to use the flag as soon as it was adopted.

he cried. But his officers were impatient; they wanted no scouting—the thing to do, they said, was to push ahead and faster. No time should be wasted. But General Herkimer was not certain. He waited. Two colonels, Fisher and Fox, became furious with the old Dutchman—they wanted no delay. They called General Herkimer a coward. This was too much for the brave general and he marched his men straight into the ambush.

Mohawks, Iroquois, and Tories sprang the trap. Fierce hand-to-hand fighting took place—first with muskets, then with bayonets, then with musket stocks, tomahawks, and knives. General Herkimer was shot in the leg and had himself propped up against a tree, where he issued orders to the hard-pressed patriots.[5] Men

---

[5] General Herkimer died from this wound.

left the fort and tried to help Herkimer's force. The Tories and Indians withdrew, leaving the Americans in command of the ravine and with the dead. Both sides suffered severely.

When the news of the attack against Fort Stanwix reached Albany, the American commander there, General Philip Schuyler, did a brave thing. Although he had few men, certainly none to spare, and in spite of the fact that Gentleman Johnny Burgoyne's army was slowly moving closer, Schuyler formed a relief expedition of nine hundred and fifty men. He placed General Benedict Arnold in command of these men and ordered him to strike for Fort Stanwix. There was no time to lose.

When Benedict Arnold's column approached the fort, a half-witted Tory, named Hans Yost, was brought before Arnold on the serious charge of spying. Patriots readied a rope and tied a hangman's knot. Arnold questioned the frightened boy and quickly realized Yost was lacking in sense. Arnold told Hans Yost that, if he went to St. Leger and told him that he had seen a huge army of Americans marching for the fort, he would not be hanged. The boy jumped at the chance to save his life. The patriots removed Hans Yost's coat, shot it full of holes, and had Yost put it on. Yost left at a dead run for St. Leger.

The Indians heard Yost tell his tale. He was wildly excited and said the Americans were as numerous "as the leaves on the trees." And besides, the American commander was Arnold, a general with a reputation.

The Iroquois and Mohawks had a terrific reaction. The Indians left. Soon the Tories decided they did not wish to fight with such a small force and they, too, withdrew from the expedition. St. Leger now considered his "army" too small and marched back out of the Mohawk Valley. This was a great relief, not only to the settlers in the valley, but for the Continental Army. One of the three forces advancing on Albany had vanished.

Chapter 14

TWO BATTLES AT SARATOGA

In the meantime, Burgoyne's unwieldy army was lumbering through the wilderness, inching toward Albany. To add to its strange appearance, the Germans were leading many pets: raccoons, foxes, bear, and deer.

The general was in no hurry. He left the lake route and built a road for his army—due south. His advance became so slow it almost stopped.

In late July, 1777, an incident happened which affected the course of the war. A beautiful girl from a Loyalist family, Jane McCrea, was on her way to the British camp to see her sweetheart, one of Burgoyne's Redcoats. She was jumped by Indians, tied to a tree, and scalped. Then her clothes were stripped from her. When the murderous Indians were certain Jane McCrea was dead, they left the scene.

The news spread rapidly through the small settlements that *no one* was safe from Burgoyne's savages, not even British sympathizers. General Burgoyne said it was a foul murder but he did not punish the Indians who did it, and the thought went about that he could not control his Indians. The American leaders publicized the murder, and many Tories, and patriots who were slow to enlist in the American Army, readied their weapons and joined up.

The American Army was looking better. All spring it had been receiving supplies from a patriot friend in France, Pierre Beaumarchais.

Burgoyne's troubles mounted. It was a Herculean job to move the heavy cannons and cumbersome wagons over the wretched road leading south from Fort Ti. American scouts began to appear and harassed the men of the circus army by musket fire. American axmen continued to chop trees in order to clog streams and trails. The time required for Burgoyne's army to travel fifteen miles from Skenesborough to Fort Edward was twenty days. And those twenty days were valuable to the Americans, for they enabled them to get their army ready for action. Soldiers from small forts like Fort Anne came out of the forts and helped to delay Burgoyne's advance.

Then Burgoyne's supplies began to run lower. Loyalists reported that there was plenty of cattle to be had for the taking in the vicinity of Manchester, Vermont. Someone suggested that the Indians be sent to bring in the beef; they were famous raiders and this would be a proper use for them. The Indians left on the raid, found some cattle, slaughtered them, and brought back the cowbells. They had devastated the country, alarmed both Tories and patriots, but they had brought back only the trophies which made a noise.

Major Skene, a Tory, told the Britisher that all he had to do to have Loyalist sympathizers flock to his colors was to make a show of force around Manchester. The town was a hundred and thirty miles away and Burgoyne decided upon a raid. He selected the German, Colonel Baum, and told him to pick six hundred and fifty men. To this force, General Burgoyne added Indians. The German, General Riedesel, advised against the raid. Burgoyne shrugged this off. The army need.

The raiders started for "Ethan Allen country." Ethan was no longer there, but two Americans in the Grants area rallied the patriots. John Langdon put up six thousand dollars and seventy hogsheads of rum for salaries and expenses, and Colonel John Stark took command. Stark was an inspiring and seasoned leader. He had fought Redcoats at Bunker Hill, in Canada, at Trenton and Princeton. There were many stories about John Stark on the frontier. When he was a boy he had experienced captivity in Canada and had been ransomed for an Indian pony worth a hundred dollars. He had been a captain in the world-famous Rogers's Rangers.

Colonel Stark was somewhat like Arnold in that he was bitter because Congress had passed him over in making promotions; but when the time to fight for the green hills of Vermont came, Stark put aside his feelings and buckled on his sword and pistols. He rallied men from New Hampshire, Massachusetts, and Vermont. It was to be a showdown fight.

When the German colonel leading the raid found that there would probably be a battle, he decided to raid Bennington rather than Manchester because Bennington was closer. The colonel sent word back that he needed more men, then he built a breastwork on a hilltop near the Walloomsac River. He placed his four cannon where they could do the most damage.

Colonel Stark led his patriots to the scene. His men drew strength from his fearlessness. Colonel Stark looked over the situation. He said, "There they are! We'll beat them tonight, or Molly Stark will be a widow."

Stark's men were not in military uniforms and when he led them toward the breastworks, the Germans thought they were the Loyalist sympathizers Major Skene had talked about. Stark and his men charged. This frightened the Indians and they ran, but the Germans were not afraid and fierce hand-to-hand fighting began. When darkness ended the battle, two hundred and seven

Germans lay dead and over seven hundred had been captured. The Americans lost thirty killed and forty wounded.

Burgoyne had not succeeded in getting the supplies and had lost about one tenth of his men.

News of the victory at Bennington spread over the northeast like wildfire. It was a tonic to the patriots. Congress finally recognized Stark's value and appointed him as a brigadier general.

But the American commander in the Albany area, General Schuyler, although he was a leader respected by many, was not anxious to face Burgoyne. General Schuyler felt that his Americans should be much stronger in numbers before he brought on a fight. He appealed to Massachusetts for aid, but he received a tart reply from old General Artemas Ward, "What can you expect us to do for you if you continue your rapid retreat and dispute not one Inch of Ground?"

Before the good news from Bennington arrived, the people in Albany were frightened. The fall of Fort Ti had been a blow. They felt that General Schuyler and General St. Clair should have defended Fort Ti to the last. A ridiculous rumor spread about the two generals: they were said to be rich from collecting *silver balls* shot into the American camps from the guns of Burgoyne.

Congress was alarmed over the feeling in and about Albany, and even George Washington was confused. Congress talked about what to do. The congressmen respected Schuyler particularly, but they thought it was time to place another leader in command at Albany. On secret written ballot they appointed General Horatio Gates to command the northern department.

The new leader was not as able as the man he displaced. However, Gates had heard the sound of bullets in battle and had smelled enemy powder, for as a young man he had fought in the British Army. Later he had settled in Virginia, and before the Revolution he made his feeling plain when he stated he was ready to risk his life for the liberty of the western world. Horatio

Gates was of medium height; he had a hawklike nose; pompous dignity; he was tactless yet kind and jolly; and he was courtly, though sometimes petty. General Gates was not a figure men adored, nor was he a daring leader.

Soon after his appointment to head George Washington's northern army, Gates wrote to Washington and told him of the supply problems he faced. Washington well knew what Horatio Gates was up against; he wrote, "One of your principal Wants —cash—will be with you by the time this reaches you."

But if General Gates had his troubles, General Burgoyne's were worse. The Britisher faced a big decision: what to do with his army. He inched farther from his base every day and his supplies were dwindling. When news of Bennington came in, followed by word of St. Leger's failure in the Mohawk Valley, Burgoyne's Indians deserted. General Howe could not help—he was headed for Philadelphia. After a council of war—and he invited the German, General Riedesel, to sit in on this one—Burgoyne rashly decided he would push ahead. Burgoyne's advance guard continued through the forest.

A farm owned by a man named Becker lay on the route of the British Army. When a Negro slave belonging to the Beckers ran to his master, gasping that he had seen the enemy, Farmer Becker gathered up his family, pigs, cattle, and buried his rakes and hoes. He moved southward as fast as he could, spreading the alarm: the British were approaching Saratoga.

General Burgoyne blundered on, handicapped because he no longer had Indians out in front as scouts. And to add to his troubles, on the morning of September 19, 1777, there was a heavy fog. Near Freeman's Farm, General Burgoyne heard the drums. At last he knew the general direction of the enemy.

At Bemis Heights, the Americans had a strong position, thanks to the engineering work of the young Polish patriot, the handsome Thaddeus Kosciusko. When Burgoyne found out about the

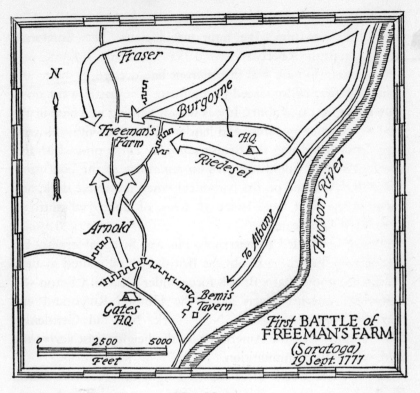

Map No. 11

heights, he ordered an attack in three columns. He himself led the center.

Burgoyne selected a poor plan. It was rough country and the three columns had difficulty keeping abreast of each other. The plan to smash the Americans was a huge gamble.

General Benedict Arnold came in fresh from the Mohawk Valley. He sought out General Gates and demanded he be permitted to attack. Finally Gates turned Arnold loose, and the woods echoed with the noise of combat. Daniel Morgan's sharpshooters were in the thick of the fight and, due to the way the fighting went, Morgan suddenly found himself almost alone.

He blew a call he had used in hunting wild turkeys and his Virginians came to him. The fight was furious. The Americans rallied against the Redcoats.

Gentleman Johnny was in the front line dressed in white and scarlet. Musket balls pierced his uniform. The battle went on at close range for three hours. It was woods fighting in which it was hard to control companies and harder still to tell who was winning. In such fighting the British *esprit de corps* proved invaluable: their units would not give up regardless of the confusion. The British camped on the battlefield when it became dark, and lying on the field were twice as many of Burgoyne's men as there were Americans.

Burgoyne decided to entrench. He was in a wilderness. He needed help. For three weeks the British general waited in vain. He did not know that a British force under General Clinton was capturing American forts along the Hudson River and was near the present Kingston, New York. Nor did Gentleman Johnny know that the Americans on the heights, just across the field, were low in ammunition.

In the three weeks after the first fight at Freeman's Farm, the American Army grew larger and ammunition was brought up from the rear. However, affairs were not peaceful in the American camp. General Arnold became jealous of Colonel Dan Morgan. Arnold threatened to resign and became so quarrelsome General Gates did not care if Arnold left or not and he ordered that Arnold would not have men to command.

In early October, with the turning of the leaves, came a great determination in American ranks; they believed they could win. On October 7, General Burgoyne decided to find out exactly what was in front of him. He sent fifteen hundred picked men to feel out the American position and determine how it could be taken. The Americans discovered the huge British scouting party and the fight started.

On this day the Baroness Riedesel was giving a dinner party

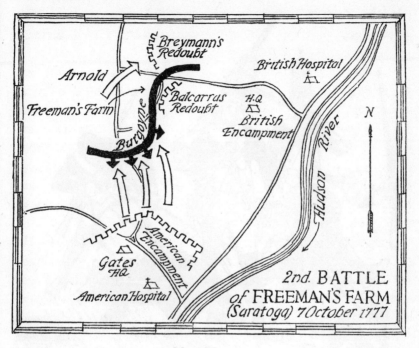

MAP No. 12

in a house she was occupying behind the lines. Generals Burgoyne, Fraser, and Philips were to dine with her. The first she knew of the battle was when painted savages went by the house, crying, "War! War!" Then, in midafternoon, General Fraser, one of the expected guests, was brought in and placed on the dining-room table, mortally wounded. The baroness took her children and servants to the cellar of the house and just in time, for shortly eleven cannon balls crashed through the dwelling. Later, it became a first-aid station for wounded British soldiers.

The fight raged back and forth. General Benedict Arnold was indignant. He had no command and no orders, and was far behind the lines—a position he had never occupied before. At about three o'clock he could stand inaction no longer. He mounted his horse and galloped into the battle. His powerful

personality and bravery inspired the Americans. He dashed
about the battlefield. He gathered up troops and led them against
the Belcarres Redoubt.[1] The fighting was face-to-face. Burgoyne's Britishers and Germans alike realized the end was close
at hand and decided to sell themselves dearly. Darkness saved
the King's army from destruction. At the instant of victory, a
Hessian sharpshooter shot Benedict Arnold in the leg.[2]

The British lost four times as many men as the Americans. The
King's army was cut off from escape and it was without food.
Finally Burgoyne surrendered and five thousand men laid down
their arms.

[1] A small fort.
[2] Writers agree that, had Benedict Arnold died here, he would have become
one of our greatest heroes.

General Gates felt sorry for the enemy and would not let the American troops witness the British and Germans piling up their arms. Gates then had the enemy generals as his guests for dinner. The Baroness Riedesel ate with her small children in a tent nearby. She said later that General Schuyler fed her and her young daughters a delicious dinner of smoked tongue, beefsteak, potatoes, bread and butter.

When Burgoyne drew his sword and handed it to the American Gates as a token of surrender, Gates agreed that Burgoyne's army would not become prisoners of war but would be returned to Europe after they had sworn not to take further part in the war. But Congress would not uphold Gates's idea of returning the British and the Germans to Europe. The men in Philadelphia were afraid Burgoyne's army would be available to fight against France or Spain, and they ordered Burgoyne's soldiers confined to prison camps. Burgoyne's forlorn men were marched to Boston, then to prisoner-of-war inclosures in Virginia, Maryland, and Pennsylvania.

There was rejoicing in Albany when news of the surrender at Saratoga arrived. Guns were fired, oxen roasted, and at night every house was illuminated. Farther down the Hudson, a British general left the Kingston area and sailed rapidly for New York City.

The American General Gates was not the hero of the battle. In 1777, with poor communications on the battlefield, it was customary for the generals to be on the field where they could personally see what was going on. They were expected to take over the leadership of troops in trouble. But Gates had remained in his tent two miles away. It was the daring battlefield leadership of Benedict Arnold and Daniel Morgan which brought victory.

The final battle at Saratoga had greater meaning than anyone present realized. It was soon to be regarded as one of the most decisive battles in the history of the world.

Chapter 15

GENERAL HOWE CAPTURES PHILADELPHIA

W HILE Gentleman Johnny Burgoyne's army lumbered through the wilderness toward Saratoga, Washington's spies could not find out where the British General Howe was going. For Washington this was a real worry. General Washington was right back where he started from: he was trying again to guess the British plan.

Because the great American leader could not find out what the Britisher, Howe, was going to do, he did the next best thing: he marched his men down from the hills at Morristown and planted himself ten miles from New Brunswick, New Jersey. Washington was now in position to give the British general battle if he started for the American forts on the Hudson, or to block him if he headed for Philadelphia.

George Washington had practically guessed the British plan. Howe wanted to capture the home of the Congress, but across the path of his eighteen thousand men were eleven thousand Americans under their best leader. General Washington's small army could probably not beat Howe's, but the Americans certainly could not be disregarded.

After some skirmishing, General Howe ordered his men to

MAP No. 13

go to Staten Island, where he placed them aboard the British fleet. Again Washington and his top officers were puzzled. *Where were the British going? What were they going to do?*

At this time, encouraging news came from the north for the Americans. They heard the results of the fighting in the Mohawk Valley and the battle at Bennington. This was wonderful, but the problem at hand for Washington and his men was the destination of the Redcoat army on the ships in New York Harbor.

When American scouts reported that the ships were disappearing over the horizon in the Atlantic, Washington thought the British Army might be sailing for Charleston, South Carolina. But

Howe sailed two hundred miles just to get around Washington's army. The Britisher ordered his men ashore at the Head of Elk in Chesapeake Bay. They had been at sea twenty-four days and the overland gain was only a few miles. As soon as he could exercise his men and horses, General Howe headed for Philadelphia.

People had been criticizing General Washington. They said he loved defensive fighting, that he was afraid to attack Howe's well-trained, well-equipped army. But General Washington was not afraid of criticism; he could stand it. He made a hurried march south across New Jersey and part of Pennsylvania to meet Howe, but again went on the defensive.

Washington took up a strong position at Chad's Ford on Brandywine Creek. Because his army was smaller than the enemy, General Washington decided to let the enemy attack.

In many battles, the so-called "fog of war," which is a nickname for uncertainty, settles over the fighting. Reports come in; so do rumors; it is hard to know what the enemy is up to. This was the way it was at Brandywine. And in addition to the fog of war, there was a real fog. No one knew where the British were.

Suddenly a farmer, who had left his home in such haste he did not have his shoes on, rode up to the woods in rear of Washington's strong position and demanded to see the commander in chief. The farmer's name was Thomas Cheyney, and he said he had important news of the British. But Washington's staff officers did not want the man to bother the general. "I am a Whig," the old farmer insisted. "I'm an American. I have news of the enemy." But the staff officers would not believe. They knew a number of Germans were to the front across the raging creek and they thought that was where the attack would come from. But Squire Thomas Cheyney shook his head. He swore he had seen British far upstream. "If you don't believe me, put me under arrest," he said. "I saw 'em. I didn't even have time

to put on my stockings. They're coming in on you from the northwest."

The old farmer was brought before Washington and the general also felt he was wrong. Washington shook his head firmly—the farmer could not be right.

Finally, mounted messengers galloped up with word that two brigades of Howe's men had circled to the northwest and were coming in behind Washington. Farmer Cheyney was right. It was a trap—the same kind of trap Howe had set on Long Island. Finally, after a two-hour fight, the Americans began to run to the rear in spite of Washington's orders.

Quickly, General Washington sent the bad news to General Nathanael Greene, the round-faced Rhode Islander, a proven leader. General Greene was far to the rear with reserve troops.

He marched them four miles in forty-nine minutes—very fast time—and met the main body of Americans, some of whom were terrified and in panic. It was the hardest kind of situation. Greene let the panic-stricken men run through his position, and then his men clashed with the enemy. General Greene's men were well disciplined and very brave. Greene's courage was contagious.

Lord Cornwallis was commanding the British brigades which had swung around to spring the trap and were now fighting General Greene's reserve troops. Three things saved the Americans from a bad defeat: the woods which had delayed and confused the British, darkness, and the leadership of General Greene.

Washington had lost more than one thousand men and he was heartbroken over the way his main body of troops had raced for the rear. But he determined to strike a surprise blow at the British and capture their wagon train. Maybe this would help offset the Battle of Brandywine.

For this he chose General "Mad" Anthony Wayne, an energetic and fearless officer who was anything but mad. Wayne made a wide march around the British to find their wagon train. But General Wayne was in trouble. He did not realize the danger spies can cause, and he allowed unknown civilians to roam in his camp at night—and he paid dearly for it.

At Paoli, Pennsylvania, the British acted on intelligence brought in from the spies who had visited with Wayne's men. The Redcoats and Germans struck Wayne's camp with a bayonet attack in the darkness. Wayne's force was badly surprised. One Hessian soldier wrote of the attack, "I struck them [with my bayonet] like so many pigs one after another, until the blood ran out of the touch-hole of my musket." Three hundred of Wayne's men had been "stuck like pigs" with the razor-sharp bayonets—the rest ran away into the night. But the British failed to capture the leader, the man with many nicknames, General Anthony Wayne.

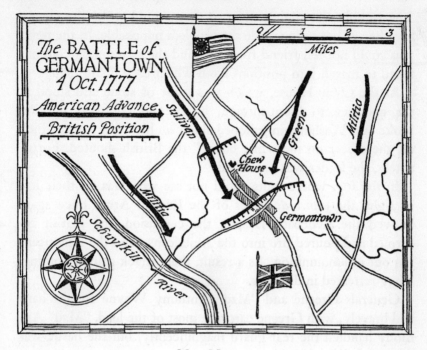

MAP No. 14

Shortly after this, the fiery Wayne rejoined General Washington. The situation was desperate again—the British were pressing on to Philadelphia. The congressmen gathered up their belongings and hurried away to Lancaster, Pennsylvania. The British marched through Valley Forge, set it on fire, then crossed the Schuylkill River and entered Philadelphia. It was September 26, 1777.

Shortly, Washington decided to attack. He would fight the nine thousand men whom General Howe had stationed north of the city at Germantown.

Washington's plan was not simple: his army was divided into four columns for a surprise march. It was night when his forces started their hike. It was difficult to control the four columns.

The trouble was timing them so they would strike the enemy together. A heavy fog made the problem impossible. In the fight, you could not tell friend from foe, and the two militia columns failed to march into positions from which they could help.

At the Chew House, which was made of stone and stood at the entrance to Germantown, heavy and confused fighting broke out. Washington galloped about on his white horse. "Pick off the officer on the white horse!" the British shouted. Fortunately, the leader was not killed.

In the fog, where units could not see who was on their left or right, the *esprit de corps* of the English Army once again buoyed the Redcoats. Despite the confusion, the British reformed and poured fire into the Americans. And the Americans ran out of ammunition. As a result, their attack gained nothing. They retreated in disorder.

Generals Greene and "Mad" Anthony Wayne fought hard and bravely, with Greene carrying most of the load. "Mad" Anthony handled the rear guard magnificently, but the battle was a bad defeat for Washington's men.

The "Year of the Three 7's" drew to a close—1777 had seen heartbreaking battles. Every thinking American knew by now that to defeat disciplined, well-trained Redcoats with troops who carried out orders only when it pleased them to do so, and who often fled when their unit seemed in danger, would be most difficult. In the American Army there was still too much desertion, sloppiness, and drunkenness to suit General Washington. Had it not been for the action in the north, the "Year of the Bloody 7's" would have been disastrous for the American cause.

Chapter 16

VALLEY FORGE AND RESULTS
OF SARATOGA

O NE can readily understand how difficult was General Washington's position. It had been a year since the victory at Trenton, and there had been heartbreaking defeats: Brandywine, Germantown, and the loss at Philadelphia. Next, the Howe brothers captured the forts along the Delaware River.[1] Washington described the latest trouble in a letter to Congress, "The enemy are now in possession of all our water defenses."

Critics began to say that General Horatio Gates, who had dazzled everyone with his victory over Gentleman Johnny Burgoyne's army, was probably a better general than Washington. The critics emphasized that Washington was strictly a defensive fighter—that he usually lost.

Congress voted thanks to General Gates and gave him a gold medal. Letters of praise poured into Congress about Gates, and Gates began to think of himself as the war's greatest general. He told Colonel Daniel Morgan that many officers in the army were ready to resign unless Washington were replaced. But Gates had talked to the wrong man. Morgan admired Washington and knew Washington faced great difficulties. Morgan was

[1] See Map No. 13, page 125.

furious. He declared he would serve under no one but General Washington. It was obvious that Gates had become excessively jealous and was almost an enemy of the commander in chief.

On the other hand, Washington felt no ill will toward Gates. When news of General Gates's splendid Saratoga victory was finally received, Washington held up his hands to heaven and gave thanks for defeat of the enemy. Then he wrote Gates and congratulated him. Later, General Washington had his forlorn army observe a day of thanksgiving in honor of General Gates and the men of Saratoga.

The question now arose, where Washington's men would spend the winter. Washington had suffered defeat. He did not have the men to fight the enemy properly, but he would not give up. He was determined to win. He would have liked to have attacked at Germantown again, but he was unable to do so. He considered taking his army to Wilmington, Delaware, where the climate was comparatively mild, but Congress protested. So Washington moved not far from Philadelphia, where Howe's army was wintering, into rugged Valley Forge.

During the fall of the year, there was serious trouble in Schoharie County, New York. Bands of Indians and Tories were on the warpath in the area north of the Catskill Mountains. With white men furnishing the brains, and the savages the cruelty, this was a terrible combination. The raids resulted in small but terrible fights. Sometimes three hundred Indians and Tories attacked two or three families totaling a dozen or so persons. Settlements were left in ruins. A large column of smoke rising above the trees became a silent signal of an Indian raid.

It was December, 1777, when news of Saratoga arrived in Paris. The victory was tremendous news for the man whose supplies helped win the battle, Pierre Beaumarchais. Ben Franklin was even happier. He and the members of his commission had worked hard and under pressure. They had attended endless conferences and discussions. Franklin's patient, unassuming ways were invaluable. He had a marvelous way of beginning a difficult conversation. "Do you think it would be a good idea," he would say. Or, "Perhaps it might be wise to consider the idea of...." Ben was humble and wise, a respected civilian who was indispensable to the cause of the colonies. The British had no representative equal to him.

Ben, and others in Paris, quickly realized the value of the Battle of Saratoga. The battle took its place among the important battles in the history of the world because it helped smash the British plan; it brought recruits and better morale to the patriot armies; it welded the colonies together; it gave Americans prestige and credit abroad; and it brought France into the struggle on the American side.

The French figured that by aiding the Americans they would make the British less powerful; they wanted revenge for their defeat in the Seven Years' War; and they believed that English trade would slump while French trade would zoom. In return for coming in on the American side, the French King insisted that the Americans promise not to make a separate peace, no matter how good or advantageous the terms.

The Tories of America were amazed that the patriots would accept aid from the French King. The Tories thought this crazy. They would almost as soon be allied with the devil; they looked on the French as traditional enemies of the English-speaking peoples.

The news of what the Battle of Saratoga and Ben Franklin's mission had accomplished in France was carried across the English Channel by spies, but the English did little although it was the most important news on the globe. In Parliament, the dying Earl of Chatham (William Pitt) dragged himself to the House and made a most dramatic speech. He scourged England for employing Germans against the colonists. He said that, if he were an American and foreign soldiers were landed in his country, he would *never* lay down his arms.

The war looked dismal to King George and his ministers. With France on the American side, the British now had to fight for their possessions in the Mediterranean, in India, and in the West Indies, as well as in North America. The British estimated they needed forty thousand men for North America alone—but where to get them? Fifteen thousand soldiers were enlisted and that was all, and most of these were raised at private expense.

The war picture may have looked black to the King, but it looked even worse to George Washington in the December of 1777 at Valley Forge.

The winter at Valley Forge was one of the most trying periods in the history of the American Army. The weather was bitter cold most of the winter and the men were half naked. They were ragged, dirty, and unkempt. Many had no shoes nor stockings. They were housed in tents and huts. Seeing his barefooted soldiers leave marks of blood when they marched in the snow would make almost any leader unhappy, and George Washington suffered. The food was very poor; weeks went by with no vegetables except potatoes. One week there was no meat, and some of the men cooked and ate leather. The men appeared at the doors of their huts at times and chanted, "No meat! No meat!" And at other times, "No bread, no soldier!" Dr. Waldo, of one of the Connecticut regiments, wrote in his diary about the thin batter of flour and water which the soldiers baked on stones before the fires:

"What have you for your dinner, boys?"
"Nothing but fire cakes and water, sir."
At night, "Gentlemen, the supper is ready."
"What is for supper, lads?"
"Fire cake and water, sir."

It was not poverty that caused the army to be fed so poorly but a breakdown of the supply system. The planning to obtain food for the army was poor, and there were few wagons to haul what food was procured. And when food did arrive, it was often spoiled by the weather. The soldiers were hungry.

Lack of food and adequate clothing brought on illness, and the sick fared poorly in the ill-ventilated huts.

The desertion problem grew worse. The British offered sixteen dollars for every American soldier who came to Philadelphia bringing his musket and who took the King's Oath.

The Continental Army was undisciplined to such an extent that, when the roll was called at formations, sometimes men were reported "present" when they were absent. George Washington was upset about this and stormed at officers who were not efficient, and some of them resigned. Washington said he was glad to get rid of unworthy officers.

Suddenly into the dark picture at Valley Forge came a soldier, a Prussian officer, General von Steuben. He was an officer of great war experience and had been talked into coming to America to help the patriots by the French war minister. He was a martinet, a tireless drillmaster, gruff in manner, yet at the same time kindly. Congress appointed him Inspector General of the Army, and George Washington gave him the job of teaching the American soldiers how to obey orders.

Von Steuben went personally to the drill field. He could do the manual of arms better than any soldier in the army. He demanded top performance from the men and got it. He accepted no excuses—yet he was human. He made the soldiers clean up. He did not mind the snow; he said it was inconvenient to drill in the snow but that it could be done. It was.

Not only did Von Steuben drill the soldiers, but he later published the first set of regulations for our army. Some of his writings are still good. He wrote:

Instructions for the Captain

A captain cannot be too careful of the company the state has committed to his charge. He must pay the greatest attention to the health of the men, their discipline, arms, accoutrements, ammunition, clothes and necessaries. His first object should be to gain the love of his men by treating them with every possible kindness and humanity. ... He should know every man in his company by name and character. He should often visit those who are sick, speak tenderly to them, see that their medicine or diet is duly administered.

Soon the spirits of the men rose. They began to consider themselves soldiers.

However, at this time, the critics of General Washington got bolder; they assailed his "habit of retreating." The people who talked against him were headed by Major General Thomas Conway, an Irish-born officer from France who had been commissioned in the American Army. Conway hinted in a letter to General Gates, the conqueror of Burgoyne, that Horatio Gates should take George Washington's place as commander in chief.

The talk against General Washington went on; both civilian and military people indulged in it. Rumors started. High officers were said to be backing Conway's idea, and the conspiracy against George Washington was labeled "The Conway Cabal."

We will probably never know all the ins-and-outs of the Conway Cabal. It is as mixed up as a kettle of eels. It is difficult to understand and even more difficult to explain.

At this time, one of General Washington's officers, General Cadwalader, felt the talk about the Conway Cabal had gone far enough. He looked upon it as an insult to George Washington. General Cadwalader challenged General Conway to a duel and wounded him. When Conway thought he was dying, he wrote a letter to George Washington apologizing, and that was the end of the Conway Cabal.

While General Washington was undergoing a trial by winter, the British were twenty miles away dancing and gambling in Philadelphia. Howe's twenty thousand men spent the winter in comfort. The Loyalist society of the town worked overtime to entertain Howe and his men. The German soldiers found sweethearts on the farms and many Germans became married.

In Philadelphia, prices skyrocketed,[2] but the social season was at its height. General Howe gambled and danced; he was little concerned about the war; he set a poor example for his soldiers.

When spring came, General Sir William Howe decided to re-

[2] Silk sold for one hundred dollars per yard; tea cost between fifty and sixty dollars a pound.

sign because he felt he had not accomplished enough. Lord George Germain accepted his resignation and sent Sir Henry Clinton to take Howe's place. But before Howe left for England he was given an odd celebration, a tournament called the Festival of Meschianza. Almost everyone in Philadelphia attended.

First, there was a water pageant featuring the rowing of boats to band music. Then, a huge lawn, over one hundred and fifty yards on a side, was lined with soldiers in full dress. High-ranking officers took their places in a grandstand. Seven selected young ladies, dressed in Turkish costume, were seated in a prominent place. Heralds blew blasts on their trumpets, and in dashed seven white knights on gray chargers. After the knights had saluted the seven young ladies, four trumpeters in black announced the arrival of seven black knights and their squires. Lances were fixed and the knights charged one another.

In the next encounter, the knights met with pistols; in the third, with swords. This display was followed by a full-dress ball in a hall decorated by eighty-five mirrors. The Meschianza seemed like a day in the Middle Ages rather than Philadelphia during the Revolutionary War in May, 1778. It was an extravagant farewell for the departing Howe. And in England, the festival was criticized. The people felt that Howe was not a great general, that he did not deserve such an affair.

Now the American promise to France of "no separate peace" was tested. The British Parliament sent three peace commissioners across the Atlantic to tell Congress that, in return for peace, the tax laws the colonists disliked would be repealed. And there would be other advantages for the Americans—everything but complete independence. Congress declined the offer. Then the three Englishmen tried to treat with the colonies separately, but were again unsuccessful.

There were rumors that a huge French fleet was sailing the

high seas, coming to help the Americans. Soon the Britisher, General Clinton, received orders to take his army to New York City, where parts of it would be shipped to fight Frenchmen in the West Indies and in Canada.

At this moment, a prisoner of war was exchanged; the erratic soldier, General Charles Lee, came back to General Washington as second in command. The return of Lee seemed to be fortunate, but it was bad luck for Washington. In a battle, Charles Lee was not a man to trust.

Chapter 17

BATTLE OF MONMOUTH

G ENERAL CHARLES LEE was glad to be back with the Americans and he soon got his chance to fight.

The British Army, ten thousand strong, was hiking across New Jersey on its way to New York. The whole countryside was filled with marching columns. Behind the Redcoats creaked an amazing wagon train, fifteen miles long. The fifteen hundred wagons were piled with all kinds of gear, and riding in the wagons or hiking alongside were women and servants. The wagons were at the head of the column, and the soldiers marched in the rear to protect them.

When Washington's scouts brought news of the train, the general held a council of war. General Charles Lee said it would be suicidal to attack the Redcoats or their wagons, which were well guarded. He did not realize the American Army had been improved by Von Steuben's drill. Almost every general in the council of war was swayed by Lee's eloquence.

It seemed a shame to General Washington to let General Sir Henry Clinton march his army to New York unhindered. The wagon train looked like an apple ripe for picking. General "Mad" Anthony Wayne alone demanded an attack. Washington thought the matter over. It was a time to risk all or nothing. Lord Marquess of Montrose had described a similar situation a hundred years before—when a leader faced a quandary—when he wrote:

> *He either fears his fate too much,*
> *Or his deserts are small,*
> *Who dare not put it to the touch,*
> *To win or lose it all.*

General Washington ordered an attack. The strike would be against the long line of wagons guarded by crack British troops. Washington asked General Lee to take a small detachment of troops and push forward to find the end of the British line. Lee sulked. He said, "That is business for a young general, *not* for the second in command!"

General Lafayette took over the command of the detachment which was scheduled to go forward. Colonel Dan Morgan and his sharpshooters were also along.

It was June, 1778, and it was hot. The temperature was at ninety-six. Troops on both sides were exhausted from the tropical heat.

Morgan's orders were to scout the enemy quietly; no shots were to be fired. He and his Virginians worked forward under cover—carefully. When British cavalry trotted by not far away, the temptation was too much for old Colonel Morgan. He ordered his men to fire. The British cavalrymen galloped away. Up rode Colonel Alexander Hamilton, an aide-de-camp to General Washington. Colonel Hamilton demanded to know who had fired.

Dan Morgan, the old sharpshooter, was heartbroken; in disgrace. He loved Washington and was mortified to have caused him displeasure. That night Washington surprised everyone. He entertained Morgan at dinner and drank a toast: "*All our friends!*" General Washington was most pleasant, and Morgan realized he was being given another chance. Morgan said later he was forgiven by Washington because it was his first offense.

The wagon train lumbered on, slowly approaching Monmouth Courthouse.[1] Charles Lee was given command of a larger force and maneuvered for battle. Wayne, the American fighter, led his men in the attack.

Young General Lafayette asked General Lee for permission to take his group and join the attack. General Lee refused. He said, "Sir, you do not know British soldiers. We cannot make a stand against them. We would be driven back. We must be cautious." But Lafayette went ahead. The battle hung in the balance.

In the excitement, General Lee saw a large group of Redcoats approaching. There was some fighting, then Lee ordered his men to retreat.

When a horseman told Washington that Lee was retreating, General Washington spurred his horse to the place of danger. The American troops were heartened by his appearance. "Long live Washington!" they shouted.

General Washington rode straight to General Charles Lee. "Sir," said Washington angrily, "I desire to know the reason for the confusion and disorder."

General Lee was stung by the words and the commander in chief's manner.

Colonel Alexander Hamilton galloped up to Lee while Lee was trying to re-form his men. "I will stay with you, General Lee," said Hamilton. "Let us die here rather than retreat."

Washington now took personal command of the battlefield. He was so excited that he broke his own rule and cursed. His orders snapped. The battle raged until six in the evening. It was not as bloody as some, but it was hard fought. There were acts of bravery on both sides. The casualties from sunstroke and heat prostration were almost as great as those from cannon fire and musketry.

[1] See Map No. 13, page 125.

In the fiercest part of the battle, Molly Pitcher, twenty-two years old, the wife of an American cannoneer, brought water to her husband while he was working at the gun. Later, when Washington heard of her bravery, he gave her a warrant as a noncommissioned officer. Like Molly Corbin at the capture of Fort Lee, Mrs. Pitcher won the praise of the men. They called her "Sergeant Molly."

When darkness came to the battlefield at Monmouth, both sides were present, but later the British slipped away to New York.

General Washington was not happy. He felt that he had had an opportunity to win over the British and that he had not taken advantage of the opportunity. He was disgusted with the experienced fighter, General Charles Lee. Now a note came from Lee, demanding that Washington apologize, followed by a letter that was insulting. Washington quickly put General Lee in arrest on the following charges:

First: Disobedience of orders in not attacking the enemy. . . .

Secondly: Misbehavior before the enemy by making an unnecessary, disorderly, and shameful retreat.

Thirdly: Disrespect to the commander in chief in two letters. . . .

Afterward, the thought spread that Lee was guilty of treachery because his retreat had helped the British.

Lee was court-martialed at New Brunswick, New Jersey, on the charges and found guilty. The affair was referred to Congress. The newspapers reflected the interest in the trial; everyone wondered what would happen to Lee.

It took months for Congress to vote on the results. Lee was sentenced not to command troops for one year. He was furious and informed Congress that he was through. He would serve no longer.

John Laurens, one of Washington's aides, challenged Charles Lee to a duel, because, Laurens said, "Lee has insulted Washington's character." Arrangements were made for a fight with pistols at five paces. The duelists fired together, on signal. Lee was nicked in the side but not seriously hurt.

Shortly, Lee disappeared from the public eye. He died in Baltimore four years later from a fever. On his deathbed, half unconscious, the great days of the adventurer's military career were uppermost in his mind. His last words were, "Stand by me, my brave grenadiers!"

Chapter 18

PRIVATEERS—AND A FRENCH FLEET

THERE was talk in the patriot army when the two high commands were getting ready to exchange General Charles Lee that Lee was scheming to help England. Whether or not this was true has never been proven. But with Lee, a man of ridiculous ego, out of the army, General Washington was better off.

In the early part of the war, George Washington used to advantage the abilities of the colonists to handle sailing vessels. The story of the privateers is exciting. It is a tale of brave men on fast ships who risked great danger for fame and money. The privateers were ships operated at private expense. Their purpose was to attack enemy commerce, and they were licensed, or commissioned, by the individual colonies or by Congress. The instructions which the captains of privateers received were very broad. For instance, here are notes on directions for American private ships of war issued by Congress over the signature of John Hancock:

I

You may, by Force of Arms, attack, subdue, and take all Ships belonging to the Inhabitants of Great Britain.

II

You may, by Force of Arms, attack, subdue, and take all ships carrying Soldiers, Arms, Gunpowder, and Provisions to the British Armies employed against the Colonies.

III

You shall bring such Ships and Vessels as you shall take, with their Guns, Rigging, etc., to some convenient Port of the United Colonies.

IV

You shall bring the Master and Pilot of every Ship you capture to Court to be examined upon Oath.

V

You shall keep and preserve every Ship and Cargo by you taken, until they shall by sentence of a Court be properly adjudged a lawful Prize.

VI

If you, or any of your Officers or Crew shall in cold Blood, kill or torture, or cruelly treat any persons on the Vessels you take, you shall be severely Punished.

VII

You shall send to Congress written accounts of Captures you shall make, as well as information and designs of the Enemy, his Fleets, and Armies.

VIII

One Third, at least, of your Company shall be Land-Men.

IX

You shall not ransom any Prisoners or Captives, but shall dispose of them in such Manner as the Congress, or Colony, shall direct.

Many privateers sold their captured prizes in European ports to the highest bidder. Privateering not only enabled a small nation without a navy to make war on the navy of a large nation, but it was a way to "get rich quick." Privateers swarmed out of every port. They became popular because a successful voyage meant wealth and fame for both owners and crew.

The great number of merchant vessels interfered with by these semi-pirate ships is hard to visualize. In the first three years of warfare, one thousand British ships had been captured; approximately eleven thousand prisoners had been taken. The loss to English merchantmen was well over ten million dollars.

There were many famous American privateersmen among the ten thousand seamen engaged in this risky business. The exploits of Captain Daniel Waters in command of the sixteen-gun ship, *Thorn*, stand out. Dan Waters was cruising about in 1776 when the lookout on his *Thorn* sighted a British troopship carrying Redcoats to America. Even though the troopship was guarded by two brigs, one mounting sixteen guns, the other eighteen, Captain Waters decided to attack. After two hours of fighting, Waters made both British men-of-war surrender; and en route to Boston with his prizes and prisoners he captured the English ship, *Spartan*, of eighteen guns. However, Captain Waters was unable to get to Boston with both of his prizes, because a crew from the sloop mounting sixteen guns overpowered a prize crew and sailed off in the night.

Another privateersman who was the talk of the colonies was Captain Silas Talbot, of the Continental Army. Talbot had followed the sea since he was a lad of twelve. He was not only a natural leader but he was also a daredevil. When he was a twenty-five-year-old army captain in 1776, he heard American rivermen on the Hudson complain bitterly about part of the British fleet anchored in the Tappan Zee. The warships, flying the Union Jack, made all river traffic obey their rules. It was "obey or be sent to the bottom."

Talbot saw rivermen in the coves along the bank building fire ships and fire rafts with which they hoped to burn the British warships. He volunteered to command the fire ship

Dangerous. To prepare the *Dangerous* for her mission, powder was spread all over the deck, turpentine was doused over combustible material. The target for the fire ship was the British ship of the line, *Asia*, sixty-four guns.

At midnight, Talbot took off all of his clothes and steered his fire ship toward the *Asia*. A rowboat followed Talbot as a means of escape. The *Dangerous* moved silently. But a young officer on watch aboard the *Asia* was alert. Guns roared and cannon balls smashed into the fire ship just before the vessels collided. Talbot struck a match. There were flames and explosions. Talbot was badly wounded and practically blinded. He leaped over the side and was rescued by friendly hands. Although Talbot's venture was not successful, the British thought the matter over and moved their ships out of the Tappan Zee.

Talbot became a daring privateersman; he not only attacked Tory shipping but British men-of-war. He sailed in the *Argo*, a ship of only one hundred tons, mounting but twelve six-pounders, and carrying a crew of sixty. His "beat" was the Rhode Island coast and Long Island Sound. Talbot showed what leadership and determination can accomplish. His men loved him, and he made them into a well-drilled team. No task was too daring for Captain Talbot, "the army privateer." He captured twelve enemy vessels, a British floating battery, and a total of three hundred prisoners.

But one day, Talbot attacked a ship, flying the Union Jack, which mounted seventy-four guns. It was the *Culloden*, a ship of the line. The *Argo* was captured and Captain Talbot found himself a prisoner bound for the dreaded Old Mill Prison in England. His privateering and army days were over.

At this time in the summer of 1778, Ethan Allen, the Vermont leader, was exchanged and returned to the American side after thirty-one months in British prisons. When Washington received and entertained him, Ethan Allen was in bad shape. After a two-day visit, Ethan left for his home in Vermont, and Washington aptly summed up the rugged personality when he wrote, "There is something in him that commands admiration . . ."

Ethan, the original speller, now sent a letter to Congress, thanking it for getting him back:

I fancy you have more Officers than soldiers, and being so Infeebeled Can Patiently recruit my Constitution Except some great and finishing Stroke is Projected in which case I would gladly attend the British with the Bayonet. . . . Their Officers affected to Treat me Very Politely the Last Two Days I was with them. . . . Their Ill Success last Campayn and our Alliance with France has Turned their Haughty Tone of Conquest to that of Love.

Congress gave Ethan an honorary promotion to colonel and saw that he received back pay, but Ethan was through for the war. He attended to "patiently recruiting his constitution" and helping the people of Vermont.

During the summer, rumors that French men-of-war would appear off the American coast proved correct. A powerful fleet under the Frenchman, Charles-Henri Count D'Estaing, appeared off New Jersey with the idea of assisting the patriots. There was great excitement as word spread throughout the colonies. Hopes were high. The colonists were in raptures over Count D'Estaing.

The count was handsome and possessed an elegant manner, but he was devoted to gambling and an easy life. He was not a great admiral. He was a man seeking fame the easy way, and he had started his American adventure with a hard cruise. His fleet had taken eighty-seven days to cross the Atlantic and his men suffered for fresh water.

The count, after corresponding with General Washington, whom he greatly admired, sailed to do battle with Admiral "Black Dick" Howe's fleet in New York Harbor, but there was no fight. The French men-of-war could not enter the harbor

because the principal vessels drew too much water to pass over the sand bar at the harbor's mouth.

George Washington conferred with the count and they decided on an expedition to Rhode Island. The object was to smash the Britishers at Newport. John Sullivan, a major general who hailed from New Hampshire, would command the land forces. He was a dignified, striking-looking officer, courageous but exceedingly blunt. He was hardly the diplomat-soldier type required to command part of a joint expedition, especially when the other commander, D'Estaing, was sensitive.

But spirits were soaring—much was expected from General Sullivan's ten thousand men and Admiral D'Estaing's fleet, which had aboard four thousand French soldiers. But shortly, every-

thing seemed to go wrong. General Sullivan's men hurried overland to Newport to be ready for the fight. But the *British* fleet
had been reinforced. It sailed out of New York and into Long
Island Sound; Admiral Howe was more anxious to fight the
French than American patriots.

The French fleet left General Sullivan and prepared for sea
battles. Then a terrific storm came up and scattered both fleets.
The best seamen were in the British fleet and they recovered
from the hurricane faster than the French. Admiral D'Estaing
now sailed for Boston to refit, but he did not even tell General
Washington where he was going.

General Sullivan's men fought well, but he and his leaders
were furious at the French for leaving. The expedition, which
had started out with such high hopes, amounted to little.

But worse, General Sullivan's fiery temperament made it difficult for the Americans to team with the French. The general
wrote a bulletin criticizing the admiral and had it read to his
troops. Sullivan said that the "desertion" of the French fleet and
the failure of the French troops hurt the honor of France.
Honor! A dangerous word to use under the circumstances. When
Admiral D'Estaing heard of this, he was angry. He accused
Sullivan of withholding information of his plans. The situation
was a mess.

Patriot leaders now saw how hard it is to work in harmony
with an ally. Not only is there the difficulty of language, but
because customs, training, and heritage are not similar there is
danger of misunderstandings.

General Washington worked to smooth ruffled tempers. It
was not easy.

And the French received a setback, for the admiral failed to
beat the British fleet when he arrived in the West Indies.

George Washington felt let down. He was unhappy over the

effort of the French admiral. It seemed as if the long looked-forward-to help from France would amount to little.

The year 1778 came to a close. The patriots' outlook for the future was bleak. Even Washington became despondent. He wrote to his friend, Gouverneur Morris, on the Council of Safety in the Continental Congress, "Can *we* carry on the war much longer?"

Chapter 19

THE BATTLE OF STONY POINT

THE cost of the war was also of great concern to every thinking patriot. Ben Franklin, still in Paris, worked every day to obtain loans for America, and he was most successful. But one of the troubles he faced was that Congress often asked him to get a loan, and before he could do so, Congress spent the money.

In order to meet expenses, the patriots printed huge quantities of paper money. This was wonderful, Franklin said slyly. He pointed out that the paper money paid for the troops, their uniforms, arms, ammunition; and then when too much paper money was printed it even paid for itself, because it became of less value.

But having paper money available did not put shoes on the feet of every American soldier. About one fifth of the army was barefooted. The ragged dress of the Continental Army was a favorite jest of the Redcoats.

In 1779, on the home front in the colonies, the cost of living zoomed higher and higher. Tea, sugar, flour, coffee, salt, pepper, and similar articles were so costly few could afford them. It was a time of inflation.

The enemy was having its troubles, too. On the march across

New Jersey, General Sir Henry Clinton lost *six hundred* men to the Americans by desertions. Most of the deserters were soldiers who married while they were stationed in Philadelphia. And, as the year 1779 progressed, a steady trickle of Redcoats left the British Army and blended into the civilian population.

The Tories were generally a disappointment to the Redcoat commanders. The British leaders expected the Tories to translate their enthusiasm for England into active service, but many of them, people of the upper strata of American society, did not take readily to field conditions and to combat. Exceptions were the Tories who combined with Indians to fight American settlers in upper New York, Pennsylvania, and Virginia, and who fought under Lieutenant Colonel Simcoe.

Simcoe's Queen's Rangers were noted for never marching at slow time, for discipline, for accurate fire with the Brown Bess, and for terrible work with the bayonet. Colonel Simcoe advertised for recruits in Rivington's *Royal Gazette* of New York City:

ALL ASPIRING HEROES

Have now an opportunity of distinguishing themselves by joining

THE QUEEN'S RANGER HUZZARS

Commanded by

Lieutenant-Colonel Simcoe

Any spirited young man will receive every encouragement, be immediately mounted on an elegant horse, and furnished with clothing and equipment.

Whoever brings a Recruit shall instantly receive TWO GUINEAS.

The Queen's Rangers was the most famous regiment in the war. It had been raised in New York and Connecticut by Colonel Robert Rogers.[1] The duties of the regiment were those of scouts and light cavalry. It had great *esprit*. The Queen's Rangers were a "flying column," used on the hardest missions. Because a man had been killed by mistake, Colonel Simcoe made his Rangers wear a peculiar black hat which distinguished them from both Americans and British.

At one period, four hundred Tories joined Colonel Simcoe's crack regiment.[2] General Clinton had need for the Queen's Rangers and every man he could command, because he planned to trap Washington.

But Washington struck first. Stony Point was the target. Stony Point is the name of a spearlike promontory jutting into the Hudson River forty miles north of New York City. It had once been an American outpost, but the British had captured it and had converted it into a strong fort.

It was time to strike. It was July, 1779. Washington could wait no longer. The situation demanded action because the former governor of New York, Tryon, was on the rampage. He had burned ships in Long Island Sound and destroyed several streets of warehouses in New Haven, where he killed a number of people. In Norwalk and Fairfield, Connecticut, William Tryon destroyed 162 homes, 142 barns, 59 stores, and 4 churches. It was time for an American counterattack.

---

[1] Robert Rogers was a well-known American frontier leader, skilled in Indian fighting. In the French and Indian War, he raised and commanded the famous Rogers's Rangers. The Rangers, like their leader, had a reputation for courage and endurance. When the Revolutionary War started, Rogers (then past middle age) offered his services to George Washington. But Washington was suspicious, because Rogers had spent so much time with the British. Washington regarded him as a spy. For part of the war, Rogers fought against the Americans. In addition to raising the Queen's Rangers, he organized the King's Rangers. Colonel Rogers lived a hard and dangerous life.

[2] Lorenzo Sabine, an authority on the Loyalists of the Revolution, estimates that during the Revolutionary War twenty-five thousand American Tories took up arms for England. The British leaders were disappointed. They expected far more would fight for the King.

For the smash against Stony Point, General Washington selected General "Mad" Anthony Wayne.

The two generals studied the fort from a high ridge a mile west of the river. Protecting them against danger was a platoon of infantrymen. Through their spy glasses, the generals saw that the rugged peninsula was not only well guarded by British soldiers and cannon, but on the land side there was a swamp. The Americans would have to wade through that swamp to get to the fort. Then in front of the guns in the embankments were felled trees and pointed stakes, with the sharp ends fixed so as to hinder an enemy. Getting into the fort would be a test for the best infantry in the world.

On the day after their look at the fort, Washington sent his instructions to Wayne:

The attack should be by the Light Infantry only, at night, with the utmost secrecy. . . . Advance with fixed bayonets and musket *unloaded*. . . . A white feather, or cockade, should be worn by our troops, and a watchword agreed on to distinguish friends from foes. . . . Secrecy is more essential than numbers. . . . If surprize takes place, the Light Infantry can do the business. . . . Keep the knowledge of your Intention to the latest hour from all but the principal officers of your corps, and from the men, till the moment of execution. . . . The usual time for exploits of this kind is a little before day. . . . These are my ideas for a surprise, but you are at liberty to depart from them. A dark night, or even a rainy one, will contribute to your success. I am, with great regard,

Dr. Sir,
Yr. Most Obet, Servant,
Go. WASHINGTON

General Wayne took another look at the ground. Taking Stony Point at night would not be easy, but he could see the wisdom for a night attack. It would be almost impossible to capture the fort in daylight.

When Wayne was ready, one thousand three hundred picked

men from Pennsylvania, Connecticut, Massachusetts, Maryland, Virginia, and North Carolina hiked toward Stony Point. These men were lightly equipped so they could march rapidly. The route of march was from Fort Montgomery (north of Stony Point), under Torn Mountain, around Bear Mountain, along a back road well away from the river.

It was black on the river road. After the soldiers had covered thirteen miles, they rested in the woods. Guards were posted to ensure that no one deserted. Again, General Wayne, with several of his oldest officers, went to a place where he could look down on the fort. Below them, the British were working to strengthen their defenses; they did not dream an attack was near.

As much as he hated to do it, General Wayne sent men ahead to kill every farmer's dog on the line of march. He wanted to make sure no dog barked and alarmed the Redcoats.

When General Wayne explained to his light infantrymen what they were to do, he offered five hundred dollars and promotion on the spot to the first soldier to enter the enemy's fort. And there were other rewards for bravery.

The men caught Wayne's enthusiasm. They were determined to win. They felt that with Wayne they could take the fort. The men were given the British rallying yell, "*The Fort's Our Own*," which Wayne had obtained from a friendly Negro.

The secret march went on, silently. There was not even the rattle of equipment as the light infantry advanced. At the narrow causeway to the peninsula, Wayne halted his soldiers. A few men were sent ahead. They seized a British sentry on watch, bound and gagged him.

In the shadows, Wayne halted the ghostly column and whispered his final orders. The group would split into two columns. The fort would be seized in a pincers movement— one column to the right, one to the left. Wayne moved forward.

The men waded the slimy swamp, muskets held high. Keep-

ing together in the darkness was a real problem. When the men were out of the swamp, they formed the two columns. "Mad" Anthony Wayne himself took the lead of the south column, which circled the shore to the right.

The Americans worked their way uphill to within pistol shot of the fort before British sentries discovered them.

Drums crashed out the alarm. Redcoat gunners sprang to their cannons and blasted grapeshot into the darkness. The Americans charged. The cry went up, *"The Fort's Our Own!"*

Wayne was wounded in the head. His aides worked their way to him through the maze of felled trees. Wayne thought he was dying. He said to his aides, "Let me die in the fort." They carried him forward. The Americans scrambled into the fort and began to use their bayonets. Soon cries went up from the garrison, "Mercy! Quarter! Quarter!"

At the end of a thirty-minute fight the British surrendered. They had lost sixty-three men. Five hundred and forty-three were taken as prisoners. The Americans had eighteen killed and eighty-three wounded. Fortunately, Wayne did not die.

The noise of the battle was heard across the river by the British at Verplancks. A Redcoat officer rowed across the Hudson to see what the noise was all about. When he discovered the fort had been captured, he got away in the darkness. As a result, General Sir Henry Clinton in New York City soon learned that he had lost the fort at Stony Point.

The taking of Stony Point was a clever victory and a needed one. There was wide rejoicing by the patriots. It was the fight of the year. The battle showed what American infantry could do under a determined leader.

Washington soon ordered the fort destroyed, stores and guns taken, and the place abandoned. He saw no reason to leave troops at Stony Point, where they could be pinched off by a similar surprise attack.

Even though the attack at Stony Point produced victory, when Washington abandoned the fort his critics bobbed up again —especially those among the Tories. They said that the rebels were seldom good fighters, and that Washington had managed to get a number of the bravest killed; that by abandoning the fort he proved that his attack amounted to little and that it was wasteful. They said he and his henchman, Wayne, had let the American soldiers act with "savage barbarity."

But Washington disregarded this. He was more concerned with a plan Major Henry (Light-Horse Harry) Lee presented. Lee said that he could capture the British garrison at Paulus Hook, New Jersey.[3]

[3] Jersey City now stands at Paulus Hook.

Light-Horse Harry Lee was aggressive and enthusiastic, but sometimes he was erratic. However, this time Washington thought Lee's plan had merit. Major Lee said that if he were given a force he could bring in two hundred Redcoats and Germans as prisoners in a hit-and-run attack. Paulus Hook was taken but not occupied.

While Stony Point and Paulus Hook had been taken in daring night attacks, affairs on the "home front" were becoming worse. Robert Morris, the Philadelphia banker ("The Financier of the Revolution"), was in trouble. People said he was making a fortune out of flour sales while American soldiers starved. Morris was mobbed, and later Tom Paine, the fiery writer, attacked him. Morris was tried and acquitted.

General Benedict Arnold, stationed in Philadelphia as military governor, was under suspicion of profiteering.

But George Washington believed in Benedict Arnold. Washington had given Arnold quiet duty in Philadelphia so that his leg, wounded at Saratoga, could mend. And as a token of his feeling toward the dashing battlefield leader, General Washington sent Arnold a pair of epaulets and a beautiful sword knot to wear on the hilt of his sword. Washington respected Arnold's ability to fight.

While Arnold was a hero to General Washington and to many soldiers, the civilians of Philadelphia suspected him. He was more interested in commerce and making money than he was in taking care of the patriots. The Pennsylvania civil authorities hated him. They discovered Arnold had made behind-the-scene deals, shady in character, with certain merchants. He became powerful. He controlled the commerce of Philadelphia. He was completely unscrupulous. He tried to keep his speculations secret, but people found out. They knew Benedict Arnold was spending huge sums. "And why," the citizens asked, "is he so friendly with the Tories?"

Chapter 20

BENEDICT ARNOLD

MAJOR GENERAL BENEDICT ARNOLD, the military governor of Philadelphia, was living in grand style on the banks of the Schuylkill River. He had purchased the most expensive house in town. He had taken as wife the blond beauty, Peggy Shippen, young belle of Philadelphia. Peggy and her father's family had many friends among the Tories, and were accustomed to move in the cream of society.

It did not take General Arnold long to maneuver so he could support lovely Peggy in her accustomed style. The Arnolds traveled about the town in a decorated coach drawn by four beautiful horses and attended by liveried footmen. At his door stood Continental Army soldiers dressed in elegant uniforms which General Arnold provided from his own purse. Shrewd observers decided that Arnold was living above the pay of a major general.

In order to get money, Arnold had become a secret partner with several merchants and he was receiving money privately in return for official favors. But in spite of his secret income, Arnold went into debt. He obtained a most unusual advance on his pay: twenty-five thousand dollars, but this was not enough.

Soon patriots in the town became critical, but there was no

curbing the military governor. He became more powerful and more autocratic. He had become a military racketeer. *What no one on the American side knew was that Arnold was in secret communication with British leaders: he was planning to become a traitor* PROVIDING *the enemy gave him enough money.*

Because he lacked the necessary tact and honesty, charges were brought against Arnold by the Council of Philadelphia. He had been military governor now for almost nine months. Some of the charges amounted to little, but the most important of them were serious and exposed his untrustworthy character.

Arnold fought back and he needed no lawyer. Dressed in a brilliant buff-and-blue uniform, the epaulets Washington had sent him gracing his shoulders, Arnold was a dramatic figure as he paraded his combat wound by limping about the courtroom. He talked of his daring leadership at Fort Ti, on the rugged march to Quebec, on Lake Champlain, at other places, and particularly at Saratoga. He described his sacrifices for the Revolution. No one dreamed he was a traitor in secret communication with the enemy.

When Arnold's sentence was announced, it was mild. He was to be reprimanded by General Washington.

The sentence was no sooner announced than Benedict Arnold resumed his behind-the-scenes speculating and sank deeper in debt. He kept telling himself that his country had treated him unfairly. The way out, the traitor figured, was to sell himself and anything that he could to the British, and the enemy was interested.

Sir Henry Clinton, the British general in New York, thought that, if he could get a high-ranking officer to desert Washington's army, the effect on the makeshift patriot army would be disastrous.

In July, 1780, General Washington decided to remove Benedict Arnold from command in Philadelphia and to give him more active duty with the army. General Arnold protested. He said that he would like a more important position, but that he was yet unable to lead in battle because of his wound received at Saratoga three years before. As a result of the conference with General Washington, the traitor soon had the job of telling his wife she was to leave Philadelphia society. She was to travel with him to West Point, New York, his new command, the strategic heart of the Colonies. Beautiful Peggy became hysterical. She looked on West Point (fifty miles up the Hudson from New York City) as being an "impossible" assignment on the crude and dangerous frontier.

Because there were no paved highways, rivers were of great importance. George Washington himself pointed out the tremendous value of the angle in the Hudson River at West Point. Here the river makes a sharp turn, and hostile ships would be under fire, almost point blank, from shore batteries. Therefore, Washington recommended to Congress in 1775 the construction of forts, batteries, and blockhouses on both sides of the Hudson River at "West Point."

In 1778, Count Kosciusko of Poland labored with the patriots to make West Point into a fortress which the enemy would hesitate to attack. It was the warehouse for extra arms and powder. Much money was spent on the defenses.

A most unusual barrier stretched across the Hudson from West Point's north shore. The patriots had mined iron ore in the hills near West Point and in their smelting furnaces had forged a long wrought-iron chain. Some of the links were forty-two inches long by twelve inches wide and about three inches thick. They weighed from one hundred to one hundred thirty pounds. The patriots floated the immense chain on large logs and guarded it with a log boom and well-placed cannon. The boom was placed on the downstream side of the chain so as to receive the first shock of an approaching ship. In addition to

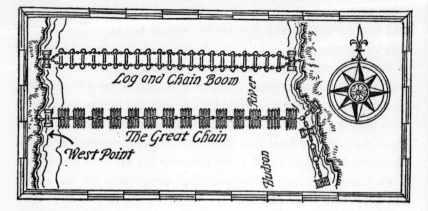

MAP No. 15

this chain and boom, another chain was located at Fort Montgomery, two and one-half miles below West Point.

Probably no warship in the world, no matter how rash its captain, could sail by the West Point defenses. The booms and chains would hold up the ship while shore guns would rake it from bowsprit to stern. West Point might be taken by land attack, but it would be suicidal for a navy to try to capture it.

Benedict Arnold arrived at West Point in August, 1780. He knew the Britisher, Sir Henry Clinton, desired to capture the fortress. Arnold established his headquarters at Robinson House on the east bank of the river, slightly south of West Point, opposite the present town of Highland Falls. The defenses of the fort needed work, but that was the last thing Arnold was interested in. He was corresponding with General Clinton and his adjutant general, Major John André, by secret code and preparing to sell the place to the enemy. He wanted hard cash.

Arnold schemed for the Redcoats to have the secret plans so that they would have the easiest possible time in taking the fort, then he would desert. Finally, the terms were agreed upon: for becoming a traitor and selling the key fortress, Arnold would receive ten thousand pounds (about fifty thousand dollars), a commission as a brigadier in the British Army, and a pension for his wife and each of his children.

The go-between from General Clinton to Benedict Arnold was the handsome, boyish Major André. Young André sailed up the Hudson on the sloop of war, *Vulture*, to meet the traitor.

At this time, General Washington saw Arnold on his way to Hartford, Connecticut. They talked a bit about the *Vulture*, a subject the handsome Arnold wished to avoid.

Two days later, wearing a dark blue cape over his scarlet uniform, Major André was rowed ashore to see Arnold. The meeting lasted until four in the morning.

Arnold took young André to a house to hide, and while they were eating breakfast they were startled by the *boom* of artillery. American cannoneers were firing at the *Vulture* and the two plotters could see the ship move down the river. It was a dangerous time for both men.

General Arnold gave Major André plans and drawings which would help the British take West Point, and a pass signed by Arnold, which would permit André to go through the American lines. John André put the valuable papers in boots beneath his stockings. Then André made a fatal mistake. He took off his scarlet coat, put on a civilian's coat, and secured a civilian's beaver hat. Because he was behind the enemy lines and out of uniform, under the rules of warfare André was now a spy.

André started out at dusk with a guide General Arnold had gotten for him. Joshua Smith was the guide, and like André, he was mounted. The two horsemen trotted toward New York, down the river trail. Beyond Peekskill, the guide left Major André, who then cantered on.

Near Tarrytown, three patriots halted Major André and demanded his pass. André produced the pass made out to *Mr. John Anderson* and said that was his name. Then André said, "Gentle-

men, I hope you belong to our party." "What party is that?" asked one of the three. "The lower party," said André, meaning the British.

The three patriots said this was their party and then André blurted out, "I am a British officer." He had talked too much.

The three men, Isaac Van Wart, John Paulding, and David Williams, searched him and found the papers. One of the three men could read a little. He studied the papers and finally said, "He's a spy!"

André tried frantically to buy his way out of the trap, but the patriots were not interested in money. They took Major André to an American colonel, who was a slow thinker. The colonel took André's suggestion and notified Benedict Arnold of the arrest! The colonel also sent word to General Washington.

But the word did not reach Washington. He arrived at the Robinson House and found that Benedict Arnold had just left for the other side of the river, saying he would be back in an hour. After General Washington and his staff had eaten, they crossed the river in a rowboat to inspect West Point. When Washington looked over the fort, he was alarmed by what he saw. The defenses were not properly manned. The east wall of Fort Putnam, high on the hill above the West Point plain, had crumbled. Two hundred men were absent across the river on a wood-cutting detail, others were stationed where they could easily be cut off. And no one had seen General Arnold. General Washington could not understand why Arnold had not met him.

The word came to General Washington of "John Anderson's" capture, with the information that he had secret papers, a pass in Arnold's handwriting, and artillery orders for the defense of West Point. There was also in the traitor's writing a careful description of "the works at West Point," as well as detailed information about the Continental Army and about assistance expected from the French fleet.

Shortly, General Washington received proof that "Mr. John Anderson" was Major André of the British Army, and that he had come ashore from H.M.S. *Vulture.*

The treason of Arnold was a shock to George Washington. He felt like Job of the Old Testament: "My soul is weary of my life.... Changes and war are against me." But Washington labored to conceal his feelings.

The general could see that the traitor had tried to scatter the garrison, to fix West Point so it could be captured. Washington issued orders for West Point to get ready for an attack by the British.

Arnold was rowed to the *Vulture* to escape. He climbed to its deck and called down to the corporal and eight privates who had rowed him to the vessel, thinking he had "business of great importance" with the enemy—which was the way Arnold put it. "Lads," said Arnold, "if you will join me, I will make sergeants or corporals of you all." The corporal at the stern of the barge replied, "No, sir, one coat is enough for me to wear at a time."

Later, Arnold sent General Washington a letter. It was an astounding attempt by Arnold to excuse his treason and it asked that his wife, Peggy, be permitted to travel to Philadelphia, or to New York, where she could join Arnold. The letter also asked General Washington to send his clothes and baggage! The commander in chief permitted an officer to travel to Philadelphia as Mrs. Arnold's escort, but that was all.

Now the spotlight centered on the daring prisoner, Major André. The British were anxious for his return. Washington had John André examined by a committee of fourteen generals. André was honest; he had nothing to hide. The generals pronounced him a spy and recommended he suffer death.

Everyone who knew young André admired him. He became a hero, unafraid to face his tragic fate. The British, and André himself, sent letters to General Washington, requesting that André's life be spared; but Washington was firm. André was tried. Under the laws of warfare, spies suffer death. A gallows was prepared at Tappan, New York. It was too bad André had to grace the gallows while Arnold, who was guilty of treachery and breach of faith, went Scot free.

On the morning of the hanging, André put on his full-dress uniform which had been sent to him: scarlet coat with green facings, buff breeches and waistcoat. In the procession to the gallows, André walked directly behind a wagon, and in that wagon was his coffin, painted black. About one thousand people were present. André climbed the wagon when it was placed under the gallows. The hangman was nervous. André put the noose in place. When asked if he had a last word to say, André replied, "I request you will witness to the world that I die like a brave man." He bandaged his own eyes. His hands and feet were tied and the wagon drove away. André was hanged. He died bravely while the traitor was comfortable in New York City.

When Sir Henry Clinton heard of the hanging, he shut himself in his room for three days. The English newspapers raged over the hanging—murder they called it.

Major Light-Horse Harry Lee now proposed a fantastic scheme. He told Washington he wanted to have the capable sergeant major, John Champe, pretend to desert the Continental Army and go to New York City. Lee believed that Sergeant Champe, a gigantic man, had the cunning and strength necessary to bring back Arnold. Washington approved of the mission. However, Sergeant Major Champe did not succeed. He arrived in New York, made the British believe he was an American deserter, but he could not get Brigadier Arnold. It was too great a task for one man.

Champe had a most difficult time, for he found himself in a force the British were sending south. It was months before he returned.

In the excitement over the great battlefield leader becoming a traitor, Washington set the example by keeping his head. He did not become mired in a bog of hate. He wrote that men must continue to believe in one another. He busied himself trying to overcome the same old problems: desertion, lack of pay, poor training of units, and the obtaining of arms and equipment for the army. He wrote Congress that in a revolution there were bound to be traitors. George Washington and the leaders under him were not stopped by the turncoat. Washington's eye fixed on the problems at hand.

General Sir Henry Clinton was sitting quietly behind the fortifications in New York City, so Congress and Washington decided to do something about the bloody raids by the Indians on the frontier.

Chapter 21

THE INDIAN FRONTIER

THE Wyoming Valley, one hundred miles northwest of Philadelphia, was border country. And in this country the Indians were the sword hanging over the heads of the pioneers. For protection against the savages, the settlers in the beautiful Pennsylvania valley built forts and blockhouses along the north branch of the Susquehanna River.

In 1778, many of the frontiersmen of Wyoming Valley were away, serving in the Continental Army. The women, children, and old men left at home were unaware that a red arrow of death was approaching. Coming through the woods toward them were Indians, Tories, British Rangers, under the infamous leader, Colonel John Butler. John Butler's cruel force struck first above the Wyoming Valley.

Blockhouses, many of which protected just a family or two, were overwhelmed. The attacks were Indian savagery at its worst. Scalps were taken. The victims were tortured and tomahawked.

In a Wyoming Valley stockade, at a place called Forty Fort, was an entirely different Butler—Colonel Zebulon Butler. He was home on leave from the Continental Army. When word came of the Indian, Tory, and British attacks, the settlers rushed for the protection of the fort. There were over five hundred rather helpless pioneers. Colonel Zebulon Butler organized them as best he could. The frontiersmen were very anxious. They knew that aid from the Continental Army was on the way, but they demanded that Colonel Zebulon Butler lead them in *attack!* Zeb Butler argued. He said it was the wrong time to attack. But Butler was overruled. The result was disastrous.

The most heartless kind of massacre took place. People were burned at the stake, others were pitchforked and roasted over red hot coals. Queen Esther, a half-breed squaw, set the example in cruelty: she worked with a hatchet. Colonel John Butler said later that his Indians took two hundred and twenty-seven scalps and carried many people into captivity while his own force lost but two Rangers and one Indian, with only eight wounded.

Chief Joseph Brant, the educated Indian, was devoted to the cause of the Tories. He was cruel, and at the head of a fierce confederacy known as the Iroquois he was a terror. The Iroquois consisted of the Mohawk, Oneida, Onondaga, Cayuga, and Seneca tribes. For over one hundred years Brant's people had received, in addition to guidance, blankets, whisky, guns, powder, flint, paint, knives, hatchets, and other presents from the English. The Indians adopted the British idea that they were the King's children. Despite the insistence of the Americans that the Indians fight on their side, eastern Indian tribes helped the British. An exception was the Oneidas.

In September, 1778, in the Mohawk Valley of New York, Chief Brant went on the rampage. At about four o'clock on a stormy night, he led his warriors into the village of German Flats and set fire to every barn and dwelling.

Then American patriots struck back at the Indian town of Unadilla, and this strike called for yet another attack by the Iroquois. This time the Indians were reinforced by more Tories.

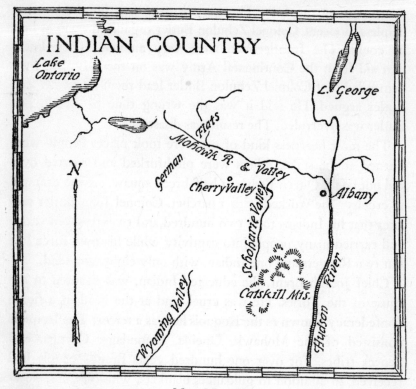

MAP NO. 16

Again German Flats and its forts were hit. The Indians and Tories burned fifty-seven barns, sixty-three houses, and carried away many horses, cattle, sheep, oxen, and killed numbers of hogs.

Warfare raged from the Mohawk to the Delaware. The frontier was drenched in blood.

Cherry Valley, only fifty miles west of Albany, had been the scene of many fights with the Indians. Now, in November, 1778, both John Butler and Chief Brant attacked. Over forty people lost their lives. Captain Ben Warren, of the Continental Army, wrote in his diary:

Nov. 13—such a shocking sight my eyes never beheld before of such savage and brutal barbarity; to see the husband mourning over his dead wife, with four dead children lying by her side, mangled, scalped, and some of the heads, some of the legs and arms cut off—twelve of one family all killed and four of them burnt in his house. *Saturday 14th.* The enemy seem to be gone; we sent out to collect what was left of cattle or anything—

John Butler, Chief Brant, and their men turned the quiet village of Cherry Valley into a smoking ash heap.

Later, an officer of the New England militia wrote of finding eight packages of scalps taken by Seneca Indians from frontier folk in New York, New Jersey, Pennsylvania, and Virginia. The scalps were sent as a present to Colonel Haldiman, governor of Canada, by James Craufurd. Craufurd wrote:

May it please your Excellency,
At the request of the Seneca chiefs, I send herewith to your Excellency, eight packs of scalps cured, dried, hooped, and painted with all the Indian triumphal marks, of which the following is invoice and explanation: *No. 1.* Containing 43 scalps of Congress soldiers killed in different skirmishes.... Also 62 of farmers, killed in their houses. ...

Craufurd quoted in his letter from a speech delivered by Chief Coneiogatchie in an Indian council:

"Father! We send you herewith many scalps, that you may see that we are not idle friends.—A blue belt.
"Father! We wish you to send these scalps over the water to the Great King that he may regard them and be refreshed, that he may see our faithfulness in destroying his enemies....
"Father! We know you will send us powder, and guns, and knives and hatchets...."

And so on with even more gruesome paragraphs. The letter closed with:

I do not doubt but that your Excellency will think it proper to give some further encouragement to these honest people [the

Senecas]. The high prices they complain of are the necessary effect of the war. Whatever presents may be sent for them through my hands shall be distributed carefully. I have the honor of being,

Your Excellency's most obedient,
And most humble servant,
JAMES CRAUFURD

There was really no "James Craufurd." The letter was a propaganda masterpiece written by old Benjamin Franklin. He did such a good job he inflamed not only Europe with his hoax but also America.

George Washington decided the time had come to follow the desires of Congress. The war would be carried into Indian country so that peace would eventually come to the bloody frontier.

On the sixth of March, 1779, Washington offered the job of commanding the expedition to General Horatio Gates, but Gates declined, which did not do him credit. Then Washington selected Major General John Sullivan for the mission. This was the same Sullivan, an officer of undaunted courage, who had insulted the French admiral, D'Estaing, in Rhode Island. Everything had gone wrong when General Sullivan had tried to team with his French ally; now Sullivan was determined to succeed.

To the people of the frontier, even more seemed at stake than fighting the British. If Sullivan failed, the move westward of the American peoples would be delayed by at least fifty years. If Sullivan's expedition succeeded, it would be one of the most important military maneuvers of the war.

George Washington now sent General Sullivan a long letter of minute instructions. The commander in chief felt he was an old hand at Indian fighting and that detailed directions would help. The first paragraph of the letter gave Sullivan his mission:

Sir—The expedition you are to command is to be directed against the Six Nations of Indians. The immediate object is their *total de-*

struction and devastation of their settlements and the capture of as many persons of every age and sex as possible. It will be essential to ruin their crops now in the ground, and prevent their planting more.

The letter closed with a strong recommendation that the general officers on the expedition inspect to make certain that no extra baggage be carried.

General Sullivan chose as his headquarters during the getting-ready period the Wyoming Valley. It was a dramatic choice, for the place was a desolate waste. Problem Number 1 presented itself: the obtaining of supplies for the expedition.

The Quakers of Pennsylvania, who were in position to furnish the bulk of the supplies, were against chastisement of the Indians. They advocated mild treatment and measures of good will. There were extremely few frontiersmen who were anxious to try good will on Colonel John Butler. Chief Brant, who was not quite as savage as Butler, was bad enough, and he had been exposed to good will at Wheelock's school in Connecticut. But when the English put pressure on Brant to fight, the kindness he learned at Wheelock's school faded.

When General Sullivan finally assembled enough rations and supplies for the expedition, Congress became disgusted at the "extravagance." The requisitions submitted by Sullivan's supply officers did not take into consideration Washington's order that no extra baggage be taken. For example, the army asked for 100 candlesticks, 254 spades, and 385 shovels.

Finally, after a long delay, which irked Washington, four thousand men started out from Wyoming up the Susquehanna. The problem was to find the Indian villages and enough Indians to fight. This was not easy, for the Indians lived in widely scattered places. The country was rough, ideal for ambush. Sullivan took no chances; his two columns had both advance and rear guards. It was an unwieldy army. On the river its baggage and artillery required many boats. There were one thousand four hundred pack horses. And the men and animals had to be fed.

The Indian villages they found were small. The first one consisted of thirty well-built houses. In the Onondaga country in the eastern part of the state of New York, the villages were not much larger. These villages were easily destroyed.

The patriots ran head-on into one raiding expedition moving toward the Mohawk Valley, and in the fight the Indian leaders were captured, tried, and hanged. Word spread among the Indians that Sullivan must be met and beaten.

Finally, the leaders of the Indians banded the tribes together. About five hundred Indians and around one thousand Tories, Rangers, and a few British Regulars took position in fortifications at Newtown, near the present city of Elmira, New York.

General Sullivan ordered the enemy position explored. Keen-eyed scouts noticed that in a certain place the trees and bushes appeared to be spaced with unusual regularity. In this way an ambush was discovered.

Sullivan sent one column through a swamp which proved to be a turning point in the attack. The Tories and Indians fought bravely, but were overwhelmed by larger numbers. It was a six-hour battle. The Indians had never fought harder; they realized their *own homes* were at stake.

The battle at Newtown was the decisive engagement of the campaign. The Indian crops were destroyed—carefully. General Sullivan estimated one hundred and sixty thousand bushels of corn were ruined. Fifteen hundred fruit trees were felled. And with winter came the result: many Indian families starved to death.

General Sullivan wanted to push on to the place at which many Indian and Tory raids had been organized, Fort Niagara, but rations for his army were scarce.[1] He withdrew to the east and

[1] Fort Niagara was near Youngstown, New York, north of Niagara Falls on Lake Ontario.

then south. Washington and Congress were delighted with the victories. The Indian question appeared solved.

But the Indians came back! In the spring Chief Joseph Brant returned to the warpath. The attacks spread to the Dutch settlements as far to the south as the Catskill Mountains in New York. The Mohawk and Schoharie valleys were next on Brant's list. The Indians learned from the whites. Not only were homes burned and people killed, but grainfields were burned black. The patriots countered as best they could, but the amazing destruction and killing continued. A Tory named Doxstader proved he could lead Indians and Tories almost as well as Colonel John Butler and be just as wanton.

The population of northern New York lived in dread. It was exposed to bloody border warfare until the very end of the Revolutionary War.

While General Sullivan was working on the problem given him by Congress and the commander in chief, the situation facing the frontiersmen in Kentucky, Virginia, and the Old Northwest Territory was bad.[2] The Indians, backed by the British, had many people frightened. But one thing was certain: most American pioneers would not abandon the land they had worked so hard to wrest from the wilderness.

The Indians had their side of the problem. The white men were taking more and more land. They paid little attention to treaties and boundaries. The result was war.

The British jumped at the situation. They did everything in their power to encourage the attacks by the Indians on the American frontiersmen. The Indians were again furnished ammunition, guns, liquor, and leadership. The British governor in the settlement at Detroit, Colonel Henry Hamilton, was believed by the

[2] The Old Northwest Territory included what is now Michigan, Ohio, Indiana, Wisconsin, and part of Minnesota.

frontiersmen to be buying American scalps from the Indians. Hamilton, the "Hair Buyer," and his scouts pointed out to the Indians how poor the colonists were. He exhibited many presents, then told the Indians his fleets of canoes would take the presents back to Montreal unless the Indians helped the British get control of the entire West.

The Americans were also endeavoring to get the Indians to fight the British; as a result, the simple Indians were thoroughly confused.

But British arms, and all that went with them, were too much for the Indians. Piercing war whoops echoed in the American settlements. The torch, the knife, and the tomahawk did their work on the settlers.

There was an aggressive young American who determined to make life on the frontier safe. He had traveled in Indian country and he felt that if he were given help he could curb lawlessness. The name of the strapping, twenty-six-year-old leader was George Rogers Clark. He became one of the greatest American frontiersmen.

Clark, the leader of the militia at the stockaded post at Harrodsburg, Kentucky, traveled to Williamsburg to lay his need before Patrick Henry, governor of Virginia. Clark asked for five hundred pounds of powder and, soon after he got it, he and eight men with him narrowly escaped capture while traveling down the Ohio River at Pittsburgh.

In early 1778, after Clark again secured the help of Patrick Henry and the Virginia Council, young Clark set out with one hundred and seventy-five men to defend Kentucky. The best way to do this, he said, was to take a lightly equipped force and strike into the heart of the West. He would not wait for the enemy to attack.

Clark's daring march through the West with such a small band could have been made only by one imbued with a forceful, magnetic brand of leadership.

Clark's flotilla of flatboats shot the Falls of the Ohio, and was rowed with the current to Fort Massac, where the French once had a fort. Here he hid his boats and set out across the level reach of the prairies and into the gloomy forests. On the fourth of July, he and his men came to the Kaskaskia River.

They had traveled on foot one hundred and twenty miles in six days and they were exhausted and hungry. Nevertheless, George Rogers Clark led his men on. He marched to Kaskaskia, a French town which had been captured by the British. When Clark captured another town, word of his raid sped to Hamilton, in Detroit.

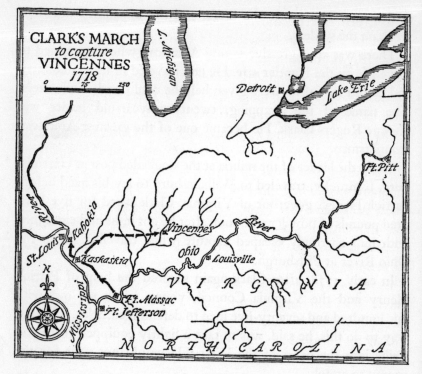

CLARK'S MARCH
to capture
VINCENNES
1778

MAP No. 17

The Hair Buyer with his whites and Indians, three hundred in number, reacted. They built a fort at the junction of the Ohio and the Mississippi and then captured the French town of Vincennes.

George Rogers Clark did not wait. He took his men in the desolate winter of February, 1779, and marched to attack the Hair Buyer. Clark counted on surprise to ovecome the greater forces of the enemy. His men forded four icy rivers. Their wet buckskins clung to their bodies in the snow, but there were buffalo to kill and eat, and Clark's magnificent spirit cheered his men as they sang and danced about campfires. He was a true leader.

The Hair Buyer and his men, snug in Vincennes, did not dream an American force would brave the wilderness in the wretched winter weather.

Clark's frame of mind is exhibited by the message he sent Patrick Henry: "... I know the case is desperate; but Sir, we must either quit the country or attack."

On the twenty-third of February, 1779, Clark reached Vincennes. He marched his men around and around a hill with drums beating; he made the enemy believe that he had over one thousand men. The Indians fled from their allies, the British; and Clark demanded that Hamilton, the Hair Buyer, surrender. At this moment, a band of Indians returned to Vincennes from a successful raid on the frontier. Clark captured them. He had six prisoners tomahawked and their bodies tossed into the river. This frightened the Hair Buyer's men and Vincennes surrendered. The American flag was run up a pole and a salute of thirteen guns fired to celebrate the victory over the British and Indians and the end of the "impossible" march.

Hamilton marched as a prisoner to Williamsburg, Virginia. George Rogers Clark wanted to strike against Detroit, but he did not have the necessary men or supplies. Later, Clark led one thousand men successfully against the Shawnees and the Delawares, who were following the renegade white man, Simon Girty. Girty was the scourge of the frontier. He could talk the language of several tribes and had been on both sides. He was well known in the forest and along the lakes for his cruelty. He set a bad example for the Indians. He was feared, hated, and despised by the whites. Girty was never taken.

The leadership of George Rogers Clark prevented the British from firmly establishing themselves in the Midwest. He dealt them and their Indian marauders a severe blow. The British turned elsewhere in search of victory.

Chapter 22

REDCOATS IN THE SOUTH

L ORD GEORGE GERMAIN, in England, and the King decided that the southern colonies should now be invaded. They believed that if pressure were applied the colonies in the south could be brought back in the British family, and that if this were done the northern colonies would become discouraged.

The trouble with this plan was that General Sir Henry Clinton could not send a huge force south. The British commander in chief felt he could spare but two Hessian battalions, some Highlanders and Loyalists, along with Irish deserters who had forsaken General Washington. The force he sent totaled only three thousand. The leader in charge, Lieutenant Colonel Campbell, realized it would be difficult to carry out the desires of the British government to invade the South.

It was a seventeen-day voyage for Colonel Campbell and his men from New York to Savannah, Georgia; and by the time they got there, the men were not in good condition to fight.

In December, 1778, Savannah, the capital of Georgia at that time, was a sleepy town of seven hundred and fifty people. On hand to repel the invaders were only seven hundred Continental soldiers and one hundred militia under the American, Robert Howe. And the defenses of the town were in poor shape.

The British hustled ashore two miles from Savannah and quickly went to work. The British light infantry, guided by a man who was helping for a reward and showed them a lonely path through a swamp, surprised the American right flank. In the attack, the Scot Highlanders hacked at the Americans with their claymores, ancient two-edged swords. The surprise fight was too much for the patriots—they abandoned Savannah.

The capture of the town was an excellent stroke for the King. Shortly, lumber, pitch, hides, and rice went out of this valuable port on the way to England.

Both sides were now reinforced. The British by the daring fighter, General Prevost; the Americans by General Ben Lincoln, a veteran of Bunker Hill. But the British had the larger force and General Prevost soon had Georgia in an iron grip. Homes, barns, and other property of the patriots were destroyed. Livestock was driven off.

Feeling in Georgia was charged with bitterness as civil war was under way. A large force of Tories marching to join the British was attacked. Seventy were condemned to death for the crime of high treason, and five of them were hanged. This infuriated large numbers of Tories; they hunted down patriots who lived in isolated sections.

The news from across the sea told that Spain had declared war against England. This spurred recruiting in England. The British fleet had even more work to do. The Americans were glad that England had to face still another enemy.

Life in Savannah went along smoothly for the Tories and Redcoats until the last day of August, 1779. On that day, lookouts on Tybee Island saw something which frightened them. Word was rushed to town that "forty-two Sail of French Ships of War in Sight." There was terrific excitement. The British in Savannah were not expecting another fight and they were not ready.

But the French admiral, D'Estaing, was in no hurry to attack the city. Although the Frenchman had six thousand troops, he preferred to *talk* about surrender—and this suited Prevost. He hoped by discussing surrender terms that they could gain time to bring in troops from outlying posts.

While the talks were going on, the American general, Lincoln, heard of the arrival of the French fleet. He hurried south with 1,350 Americans to join with the French in the attack.

But the British delayed Lincoln by destroying bridges in his path. They also sank vessels in the Savannah River to hinder the movement of the French fleet and, while the talks went on and on, they built better fortifications.

Finally, a French warship of twenty-eight guns began to throw shot and shell into the town. The battle began. When the Americans and French attacked Savannah, the famous Sergeant Jasper of South Carolina, the hero of Fort Moultrie in 1776, was one of a small group who determined to plant the colors on the British lines. He was wounded twice and died as a result. Among the wounded were Count D'Estaing and Count Pulaski.[1] The allies retreated, "shamefully," a British newspaper reported.

The French admiral now declared he would leave with his fleet. This was a blow to the Americans, who demanded the French remain. In no time the allies were quarreling. The French admiral became excited and pointed out that an American sergeant major had deserted and had given the plans to the enemy. This was correct. The two allies were angry at each other again. It was Newport repeating itself.

Admiral D'Estaing ordered his warships to raise anchors. He

[1] Pulaski died of this wound.

sailed away, leaving Georgia in British hands. The Americans could not understand such a move.

Things looked bad for the patriots' cause. This made the Loyalists very happy.

But the British in America were bothered by Lord Germain, whose orders were often not smart. He called for raids here, raids there, with little thought given to the numbers of troops or to supplies. Germain wanted Sir Henry Clinton to attack George Washington, and at the same time he wanted the patriots in Carolina squelched. This was the spring of 1780.

Sir Henry Clinton had enough of this interference and tried to resign. He submitted his resignation twice, but Germain and the King would have none of it. Finally, Sir Henry himself led an expedition to the south. The strike was against Charleston, the capital of South Carolina.

When Sir Henry sailed south with a mass of ships and eighty-six hundred soldiers, he had no worries about American ships, and his other enemy, the French, had sailed their fleet back to France. The biggest trouble facing Sir Henry was the stormy Atlantic. In the gales off the North Carolina coast his ships were almost wrecked, and many of his artillery and cavalry horses died. It took a month for his ships to make the voyage to Charleston.

Having learned from his experience of 1776, Sir Henry Clinton approached the town of Charleston from the land side. Once again there was extreme excitement in the city. Reinforcements from the north swelled Sir Henry's attackers to fourteen thousand. The American general, Lincoln, shut up in Charleston, was outnumbered two to one, even though General Washington sent seven hundred men. The outlook for Lincoln and his men was black.

On the Redcoat side, the hopes of General Sir Henry Clinton were high. He believed that by dealing the South Carolinian patriots a deathblow at Charleston he could present South Carolina

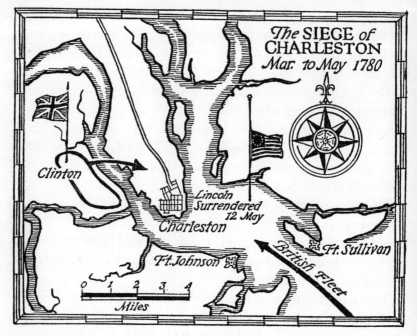

MAP No. 18

to the King. He felt hundreds of Tories in the colony would join his colors if he could win.

Governor Rutledge, of South Carolina, worked every available man and hundreds of slaves to get ready the defenses of the town. The pressure was on. A great disappointment to him was that the militia would not help; they feared smallpox and would not come into the town.

Sir Henry ordered his soldiers to dig zigzag approach trenches toward the American breastworks. Despite patriot cannon fire, which blasted the trenches and showered the Redcoats with dirt, the British worked closer and closer.

In the attack on Charleston, Sir Henry had the benefit of daring leadership from a stockily built horseman, Banastre Tarleton. Ban Tarleton, twenty-six, was a lieutenant colonel, and he possessed great energy. He believed in striking fast, in killing any patriots who got in his way. He scoured the country for farm horses to replace those lost at sea. The Tories in his command were devoted to him. He soon captured better horses for his men than the slow farm horses. While Sir Henry put a stranglehold on the town, the daring Ban Tarleton controlled outlying districts to make sure that General Lincoln got no reinforcements. To add to the general's woes, the British fleet sailed by Fort Moultrie. Charleston was in desperate straits; it was under attack from two sides, by land and sea. Cannon balls plowed through the buildings.

General Lincoln was up and down the front lines cheering his men. But finally food gave out. He asked for surrender terms. A harsh reply came back—there were no terms, nothing but complete surrender.

General Lincoln saw no hope and gave up. Fifty-five hundred patriots laid down their arms. In addition, one thousand American and French seamen were captured. The British gained four hundred cannon. For the patriots, this was one of the worst defeats of the war.

Now the fearful dragoon, Tarleton, rode at top speed with his men for a beautiful district near the North Carolina border known as the Waxhaws. The American commander there was surprised. He showed a white flag. This meant nothing to Tarleton. He overrode the Americans and slaughtered them. The patriot commander cried, *"Mercy! Quarter! Quarter!"* The British answer was a slash of cavalry sabers. One hundred and thirteen Americans were killed, hundreds more were wounded. Tarleton was so cruel that the term "Tarleton's Quarter" was used from then on to denote the killing of helpless men who want to surrender.

General Sir Henry Clinton now sailed for New York and left

his fellow Englishman, General Cornwallis, to follow up the
victory at Charleston.

The civil war in the Carolinas became more ruthless. Part of
the blame can be placed on Tarleton's bloody action in the Waxhaws. American guerrillas, led by daring men, Brigadier General
Thomas Sumter, Andrew Pickens, and Lieutenant Colonel Francis Marion, gave the Tories and British no rest.

Marion, known as the "Swamp Fox" because he took refuge in

the swamps and because he was so smart, was small in stature. They said "he was not larger than a lobster and might easily be placed into a quart pot." The Swamp Fox in 1780 was forty-eight years old. He was a man of few words and of great action. His followers adored him in spite of his rigid discipline. He was unselfish and fearless. He *sought* danger. Sometimes his band consisted of thirty privates, sometimes less. Often they had little ammunition. They seldom had blankets; they slept on pine needles. Coffee for breakfast was a luxury. Marion himself liked the drink of the Roman soldier, vinegar and water.

Marion's men believed in him. They attacked headlong at his order when he thought they had a chance to win. He utilized surprise, and when he was overwhelmed he and his riders disappeared in the swamps. Lord Cornwallis dispatched his ace dragoon, Tarleton, to bring in Marion; but Tarleton was unsuccessful. Marion was a virtual will-o'-the-wisp.

Once, word came to Marion's hiding place in a swamp that one of his scouts had observed the British taking American prisoners to Charleston. "There are about two hundred prisoners," said the scout.

"How many guards?" asked Marion.

"Ninety, sir."

Marion and thirty men trailed the British party to an inn, where it halted for the night. Later, when Marion heard songs from the tavern, he attacked. The sentinels gave the alarm, but Marion overpowered them and set the prisoners free, killing but three men. The British captain was found hiding up a chimney. This capture at Blue House Tavern is an example of the trouble which Marion's leadership caused the British.

On another occasion, a young British officer was led blindfolded into the swamp to talk to Marion about exchanging prisoners. When the blindfold was removed, the Britisher was amazed to see that sweet potatoes cooking on the ashes were the only food. When the potatoes were served on bark to the men about the campfire, the Britisher said, "I suppose this is an accidental meal. I am sure you live better than this."

"No," said Marion, "we often fare much worse."

"But I suppose you are paid well?"

"Not a cent, sir," said Marion.

Later, the British officer said he had seen an American general and his men without pay, dressed in rags, living on roots. "What chance," he said, "have we against such men?"

The American people loved tales about Marion. Later, William Cullen Bryant wrote "Song of Marion's Men." It began:

> Our band is few, but true and tried,
>   Our leader frank and bold.
> The British soldier trembles
>   When MARION'S name is told.

The poem tells of his action at night:

> Well knows the fair and friendly moon
>   The band that MARION leads,
> The glitter of their rifles,
>   The scampering of their steeds.

The Swamp Fox struck terror to the hearts of Tories; to the patriots, he was a romantic hero; to the British, he was a daring enemy whose light troops could be expected to attack any place, at any hour.

Now came a surprise for Washington: out of a clear sky, Congress appointed General Horatio Gates, the hero of the Battle of Saratoga, to command the Americans in the south. Congress did not ask Washington about this. It merely told Gates to take command. Washington was careful not to show his feelings.

General Gates arrived by horseback in the south. He took a quick look around and his English background asserted itself —he was contemptuous of the American troops. Supplies were low. Nevertheless, he decided to rush ahead even though he knew nothing of the enemy. He ordered a march for Camden, in the northern part of South Carolina; he hoped to mop the British up there. But the trouble was, he was up against Lord Cornwallis, a wiser and better general than the general whom Gates had defeated at Saratoga: Burgoyne.

The two armies clashed near Camden, South Carolina, on a narrow plain between two arms of Gum Swamp. The British were well informed about Gates's men. Amazingly enough, General Gates now learned that in his own army he had three thousand men, *not* the seven thousand he thought he had.

A brave officer fighting under Gates, Major General DeKalb, a German by birth and a French Army veteran, was not panicky when the Redcoats overwhelmed the Americans. General DeKalb formed his Continentals and for a while kept the British bayonets away. But DeKalb was wounded eleven times and died.

When his victory was won, General Cornwallis put the fearful Ban Tarleton and his dashing cavalrymen into the fight. Tarleton's horsemen pursued and killed Americans, who were running for their lives, for thirty miles. Patriots who hid in the swamps escaped. American baggage and ammunition wagons were captured. There was confusion everywhere on the American side, for there was no real commander on the battlefield. As fast as Tarleton was, he was unable to catch Gates. Gates made two hundred miles on horseback in three and one-half days' time. He finally gathered up eight hundred of his men, a pitifully small remnant, but he had suffered a bad defeat. He was finished as an army leader.

Cornwallis now gripped the Carolinas. He wrote a terse message to one of his colonels:

August, 1780

I have given orders that all inhabitants who have taken part in this revolt should be punished ... their whole property taken from them or destroyed. . . . I have ordered that every militiaman, who has borne arms with us, and afterwards joined the enemy, *shall be hanged.* . . . I desire you to punish the rebels.

The atrocities authorized by General Cornwallis made the war almost unbearable in the south. The British and Tories far exceeded the orders of the British fighter.

Marion rode out of his swamps at the head of his intrepid band and harried the enemy. The result of his effort was small, but he made a wise remark about the future. He said that, while the medicine being administered by the Tories and British was bitter, it would eventually cure the south of Toryism. But the morale of the southern patriots sank to zero.

Chapter 23

MISERY AND MUTINY

DEFEAT in the south was not the only discouraging thing to the patriots. The British had become stronger on the ocean and blockaded the coast. They raided New Haven and Norwalk, Connecticut, looted and set fire to hundreds of buildings—even churches—and they also devastated property in Virginia. The treason of Arnold made men wonder if other high commanders were untrustworthy. Enthusiasm for revolution was on the wane. It looked as if Lord George Germain would soon be able to tell the King, "The American rebels are exhausted. Soon all the colonies will be once again under your control."

Patriot leaders were handicapped by the worthless currency. The expression "not worth a Continental" meant that the object referred to was valueless, like the money of the Continental government.

Bravery and protection could be paid for in currency, providing the money was sound, but payment to the soldiers in the form of small amounts of goods and food was not practical. Corn cost one hundred and fifty dollars a bushel. It took sixty dollars worth of Continental money to equal one dollar in coin. Another currency system was tried but it, too, failed. The private soldiers were in bad straits: four months' pay would not buy a bushel of wheat.

Men in the service who were heads of families were worried about starvation of their loved ones at home, but they were not allowed to leave the army. Consequently, desertion increased, to the delight of the enemy and the Tories. Some troops had gone four months, five months, others six, without pay. They could not even get pay in worthless money.

Great difficulty was experienced by the Quartermaster Corps in feeding the Continental Army, because the states were slow furnishing supplies.

Another hard winter was close by when George Washington moved the army to Morristown, New Jersey. Most of the men arrived in the area on December 5, 1779. Before they could put up a log-house city, cold weather blew in, and it was a case of working in the snow and sleeping under canvas on frozen ground. In the records of the army, 2,898 men were marked unfit for duty because they were barefoot or "otherwise naked." The hardships at Morristown that winter were worse than those at Valley Forge.

General Knox, the artillery chief, was greatly concerned over lack of food for the horses which would be expected to pull the guns when spring came. General Nathanael Greene, the Quartermaster General, also worried because the supply-wagon horses were almost starving. Once, General Greene reported that he did not have one ton of hay available. Had it not been for the citizens of New Jersey, who responded to an appeal from George Washington, the army of four thousand men and many horses would have starved.

A new difficulty now appeared; some of the states began to compete for enlistments with the Continental Army by offering a bounty of one thousand dollars over the sum provided by Congress. The "bounty jumpers" became active again, enlisting in one state, collecting the fee, then deserting to enlist elsewhere in order to collect more money.

Jealousies plagued Washington and Congress. Colonel Dan Morgan, who was born in New Jersey but who hailed from Virginia, protested about lack of promotion before the Battle of Camden. Morgan could laugh over the time, when he was a young teamster in the British Army, when he was sentenced to be stroked with the cat-o'-nine-tails five hundred times. The drummer had miscounted and he received *only* 499. But Colonel Morgan's sense of humor deserted him when Congress promoted junior officers over his head. He resigned. Washington was greatly disappointed in him. Congress knew Morgan was a winner and ordered him back into the army, but Morgan would not budge from his home. But after Gates's defeat at Camden, the giant came back of his own free will.

There was much work to be done in the south. The defeat of Horatio Gates at Camden left little semblance of an army and had removed glamour from his name. Now Congress asked General Washington to straighten out the mess, although it had not consulted the commander in chief when Gates was placed in command of southern patriots.

Washington appointed one of the best generals of the Revolutionary Army to command in the Carolinas: Nathanael Greene, leader from Rhode Island. Greene, son of a Quaker preacher, was brave, cheerful, and smart.

The Marquis de Lafayette now returned to America with what looked like good news. He told his friend, General Washington, that the French fleet was coming back. Washington was determined that this time a better effort would be made to work with the French. But in July, 1780, when the French armada returned, there was disappointment; the French fleet was not large, but it had many French soldiers aboard. The British acted fast and soon blockaded it in Newport.

Jealousy boiled to the top again. The stanch and popular artillery chief, Henry Knox, became enraged because another was promoted to major general ahead of him. Washington warned Congress that things like this upset almost everyone.

Now something happened which shook the already wavering Revolutionary Army: some of the soldiers in the wretched huts in the Morristown camp mutinied.

The American Army was in a miserable condition.

This was a serious riot. Thirteen hundred men were involved. The mutiny began on New Year's Day, 1781. At nine o'clock at night, Pennsylvania troops began to shout and fire their muskets. They shot a captain through the head and wounded another. A lieutenant tried to quiet the men and was wounded in the leg. One of the soldiers went down—shot. General "Mad" Anthony arrived on the scene and talked to the men. The mutineers then went for the cannons.

General Wayne tore open his uniform and bared his breast. "If you mean to kill me, shoot me at once," he said. But the men disregarded Wayne; they elected their sergeants as leaders and started marching for Philadelphia to see Congress. They said they wanted their wrongs "straightened out."

General Wayne wrote a hurried letter, warning General Washington, and sent it by express rider to New Windsor, near West Point, New York, where Washington was staying. Washington was torn between going to the mutiny and taking charge in person or staying in the West Point area which might be attacked. He chose the latter.

In the meantime, the mutineers marched into the small village of Princeton and dominated the town. They met with Wayne and two colonels, and demanded that men who had long served be paid and discharged. They further insisted that the recruits with them be paid and allowed to return to their regiments, and that no "grievances" be held against any mutineer. Wayne wisely

said the decision was up to the Pennsylvania Assembly and to Congress.

Spies reported the mutiny to General Clinton in New York City. The British leaped to take advantage of the situation, hoping that more men would mutiny. Sir Henry Clinton sent two agents to Princeton to talk to the mutineers and to persuade them to come over to the British side, where they would be paid and clothed properly.

But the American mutineers surprised everyone in the village by handing over the two agents to General Wayne with the recommendation that they be hanged. The mutineers said they would obey General Wayne, whom they adored, and wanted no reward except "the love of our country," and they said they would fight the British.

Joseph Reed, the president of Congress, and authorities from Pennsylvania came to talk to the mutineers.

The warmhearted General Wayne, in an effort to win the mutineers back to the army, offered a reward to the mutineers who had handed over the British agents. But the mutineers refused to take the money.

The result of the insurrection was victory for the mutineers. More than half of them were released from the army, and the rest placed on furlough. The civilians who were in on the settlement ended up by admiring many of the men who had revolted.

The trouble was that the result of the mutiny encouraged another revolt. The New Jersey troops at Pompton now revolted. Although this was a smaller affair, George Washington decided it was a crisis. The time had come, he believed, to determine whether or not soldiers would be soldiers, and whether or not there would be an army to fight the British.

Washington took no chances. He ordered the American general, Robert Howe, to surround the two hundred mutineers with five hundred other soldiers. A court-martial was held in the field. Two ringleaders were shot with the rest looking on. The army learned that mutiny was bad business.

Washington wrote a General Order, "We began a contest for liberty ill provided with the means for the war, relying on our patriotism to supply the deficiency. We expected to encounter many wants and distresses.... We must bear the present evils with fortitude...."

But General Washington wondered if both the army and the people on the home front were losing heart.

Chapter 24

THE STRANGE BATTLE AT KINGS
MOUNTAIN–FIGHT AT COWPENS

THE defeat at Camden was a terrible blow to the patriots, for it put the British in position to mop up the southern colonies.

But the patriots of North Carolina were far from downhearted. The war was not so black but that they could tell stories about it. They told of how Sam Clowney, a quick-witted native of Ireland, and a Negro friend named Paul were near Cedar Spring when they saw five Tories gallop through the woods to a creek. Clowney put the Negro in the bushes and went forward. He yelled to the five Tories that they were captured, and that if they did not surrender they would be killed. Then Clowney called to his friend in the bushes, "Cock your guns, boys, and fire at my word!" When Clowney marched his five prisoners back to his colonel, he gave commands to his "troops" in the bushes. "Right about wheel!" he shouted. "Forward! Guide right!" Colonel Thomas, in command in that area, was amazed, and asked Clowney how he had performed such a feat.

"May it please Your Honor," said Clowney, "*I surrounded them!*"

Feeling ran high among the backwoodsmen and trappers in

what is now Tennessee, West Virginia, and southwestern Virginia. For instance, along the frontier, a young lady would not let a boy call on her unless he had volunteered in the defense of his country.

The Tories, encouraged by the battle at Camden, decided to stamp out patriot enthusiasm and guerrilla activities in North Carolina. Cornwallis sent a force of Tories through the foothills of the Allegheny Mountains. The Tories were completely organized and equipped. The British called them "The American Volunteers."

The leader of this Tory expedition was the best rifleman in the British Army, Major Patrick Ferguson. Ferguson's hobby was firearms. He had invented a breech-loading rifle which fired a new-type pointed bullet. Once, in demonstrating the worth of his rifle to British Army authorities, he prepared the rifle for firing, then poured a bottle of water down the barrel and into the pan to drench the powder. In half a minute, without taking the bullet out of the barrel or putting in dry powder, he fired the piece. Pat Ferguson was also a fine marksman, and with his new rifle he could lie on his back and hit a bull's-eye one hundred yards away.

In addition to being a small-arms expert and an inventor, Pat Ferguson was a brave and determined leader. He was thirty-six years of age, of athletic build. Pat had been in the army since he was fifteen, and had served in combat. He had been wounded in the arm, and when he fought with his sword he used his left hand. He was ruthless in battle, but he had a higher code toward the vanquished than Ban Tarleton. The men under Ferguson had confidence in his leadership.

Pat Ferguson led his American Volunteers into North Carolina from South Carolina, sending word ahead by a prisoner that if the people did not stop their opposition to the King "he would march his army over the mountains, hang their leaders, and lay the 'Old North Country' in waste with fire and sword."

This was not the kind of talk that would pacify the North Carolina back-country settlers. It had the opposite effect. It made the patriots believe the news of British atrocities. Now, the prediction of the Swamp Fox was about to come true: outrages committed by the British and Tories would strengthen the patriots. One thousand half-wild frontiersmen, many of Scotch-Irish descent, decided the time had arrived for a showdown fight.

The mountain men assembled near the present site of Elizabethton, Tennessee. They were as tough as Indians, and not easy to control. These frontiersmen were under several natural leaders: Colonels Isaac Shelby, William Campbell, "Nolichucky

Jack" Sevier, and Ben Cleveland. More settlers came. The force
was now over three thousand.

When Major Pat Ferguson found out he was marching into
a huge hornets' nest he sent word to Lord Cornwallis and retreated across the boundary between the two Carolinas and set
up a fortified camp on top of Kings Mountain.[1] Ferguson sent
messengers to gather up more Tories. Dispatch riders tore south
to Lord Cornwallis, asking for help, but it was too late.

The American mountain men arrived at Kings Mountain on
the warpath, traveling light. Their uniform was the dress of the
frontier: hunting shirt and buckskin trousers or breeches. They
reined their horses up and dismounted. The word was passed
down the line, "Tie up overcoats, pick touch-holes, fresh prime,
and be ready to fight!" Colonel Cleveland talked to the men, "I
will show you, by my example, how to fight."

The British were in a strong position, but the backwoodsmen
did not stop. The Americans practically surrounded the rocky
hill and marched carefully up its slopes and wooded ravines. It
was slaughter with Tories on the losing end. In the face-to-face
fighting, the patriots yelled, "Tarleton's Quarter!" Practically
none of Ferguson's men escaped death or capture and, at the end
of the battle, the famous British rifleman himself lay dead.

The way in which the war divided North Carolina country
was demonstrated in this battle by the four Logan brothers.
William and Joseph fought on the patriot side, John and Thomas
under Pat Ferguson. William was killed during the march up the
mountain. Thomas had his thigh badly shattered, and John was
taken prisoner.

"Long Sam" Abney of Edgefield, South Carolina, who survived the battle, liked to tell in his old age how he was a patriot,
but when Charleston fell he put himself under British protection.
The British construed this to mean that he was available to fight

[1] See Map No. 19, page 208.

in their army and impressed him in Ferguson's corps. In the battle at Kings Mountain, Long Sam took cover behind a rock but decided he would not shoot his friends. Soon a musket ball struck him in the fleshy part of his arm and he said this made him "a little mad." A few moments later, he was wounded again and he said this made him "mighty mad." He then started to aim carefully at his friends, and the record states, he "fought with bravery." Long Sam Abney was wounded seven times in the battle but survived.

The morning after the battle, the frontiersmen started home with six hundred prisoners. They stopped long enough to hold a court-martial and hang nine Tories who were guilty of robbery and worse crimes. Then the backwoodsmen decided that they had done enough: *their* area was cleared of the King's men. So they all went home, except a few who guarded the prisoners. This hard-fought engagement was the strangest battle of the war, for a day or so after it the patriot force disappeared.

In Cornwallis's words, "Our defeat was a very unexpected and severe blow." It made Cornwallis alter his plans for a march north, for he soon learned that the North Carolina Tories were cowed and would not help him. The Battle of Kings Mountain had a far-reaching effect.

The plan to conquer North Carolina was abandoned. Soon patriot guerrillas were on the roads and trails again after other Tories. Lord Cornwallis loosened his hold on the village of Charlotte, North Carolina. An amusing result was the reaction when the news arrived in General Sir Henry Clinton's headquarters in New York City: the officers there would not admit that the battle had ever taken place.

It was at this time that George Washington decided to try to help affairs in the south by giving this tremendous job to General Nathanael Greene. Nat Greene found perfect chaos when he arrived at Charlotte. General Gates's defeat at Camden had left affairs in the worst possible condition. Greene had received many promises of help, from Congress, from General Knox (the artillery chief), from authorities in Maryland, Virginia, and Delaware, but General Greene observed few results. He faced a big task.

The patriot "army," which this fine general from Rhode Island found at Charlotte, was without weapons, ammunition, clothing, and was half-starved. Despite the victory of the backwoods militia at Kings Mountain, the spirit of the American fighting men whom General Greene inherited was gone.

There were only eight hundred men fit for service although the paper work showed the general had three thousand four hundred men present for duty. And many of the men said to be ready were poorly disciplined. There were few cannon. The country around Charlotte had been devastated, and supplies were scarce. The Americans were in a sad state of affairs.

Greene first talked to his best officers. After a council of war, he decided to move his men to a place on the Pee Dee River, in the northern part of South Carolina. He thought he would be unmolested and could train his army there, and that drill would give his men better discipline. There was also the probability that in another area they could get better food.

Greene was determined not to make Gates's mistake and rush off pell-mell and fight windmills suddenly to find the windmills overpowering. He wanted to know about the country in which he might have to fight, so he sent out two mapping parties; one of these was commanded by a general: Kosciusko.

Greene sent Dan Morgan, now a brigadier general, with a few hundred troops to Winnsboro, just above the center of the state, where Cornwallis had his British Army. Morgan was perfectly suited to the job of scouting the enemy and striking when he had the chance. With General Morgan was the Swamp Fox and

Lieutenant Colonel Henry Lee's crack horsemen known as "The Legion."

There were terrific leaders on the British side, too. Lord Cornwallis was much more aggressive than the average British general, and commanding his horsemen was the man whose name was being used to scare Carolina children: Ban Tarleton.

Lord Cornwallis sent Tarleton to crush General Morgan.

Tarleton found Morgan on the seventeenth of January, 1781, at a place west of Kings Mountain known as the Cowpens.[2]

Tarleton, the dashing leader of light and fast-striking Redcoats, felt he had Dan Morgan trapped, for behind the Old Wagoner was an unpassable river. Dan Morgan appeared to be in a bad fix.

But Morgan was not frightened. He had been in worse places: for instance, the valley near Fort Pitt where Indians had surprised and had chewed up General Braddock.

The night before the battle, the Old Wagoner visited his men about the campfires; his confidence reassured them. His attitude was contagious. He talked of the battle due the next day. "Give me two fires at killing distance," he said, "and I will make victory sure."

Morgan made certain everyone on his side understood his plan so there would be no panic.

When Tarleton's Redcoats advanced with their artillery blasting away, and his fearful dragoons on both flanks, he and his men were tricked by Morgan. After firing twice, Morgan's first line of Americans gave way and ran behind the second line, reforming behind a hill as a reserve.

Tarleton's men saw the "retreat" and thought they had won the fight. But they were met by another deadly volley. Tarleton's horsemen thundered on. Now Morgan's own dragoons swept from the flank into the battle. The British dragoons were sur-

[2] See Map No. 19, page 208.

prised. Out from behind the hill came Morgan's reserve in a bayonet charge. This was too much; the British were through.

Tarleton's loss at Cowpens was seven hundred killed, wounded, or captured. The British also lost two cannon, eight hundred muskets, a baggage train of many wagons, tents, ammunition, and their colors. Colonel Tarleton himself escaped with a few men. Almost as important to the Americans as the captured equipment was that Tarleton was no longer a scary legend. This battle was a victory comparable to the win in the north at Bennington.

But as happy as Dan Morgan was, he could not afford to rest his weary men, for Cornwallis was nearby. Morgan ordered the hogsheads of captured whisky in the British baggage train smashed so his men would not be tempted, then he marched his men swiftly toward General Greene.

Cornwallis tried to trap the Old Wagoner but did not move fast enough.

Lord Cornwallis was not a quitter. This stern man was the best of the British generals. He was not personally upset by the tide of events. He wrote General Clinton in New York that he would continue to operate; he would fight on and smash the rebels.

The first thing Cornwallis did was to burn his baggage and most of the wagons. This was a most courageous decision. If the rebels could move rapidly (because they had only bare necessities with them), he would be a match for them. Gentleman Johnny Burgoyne had come down from Canada four years before with a baggage train that hindered his army. There would be nothing like that to hamper Lord Cornwallis. He kept only four wagons for the sick and wounded, and a few more for medicine, ammunition, and salt. Cornwallis stripped down for a killing fight. He was determined to overcome Greene's little army.

Chapter 25

A NINE-HUNDRED-MILE MARCH
TO VICTORY

G ENERAL NAT GREENE now faced the question: what should the Americans do to further their cause? The Old Wagoner gave his advice. Morgan said that it was best to strike west for the mountains, that Cornwallis would not dare to bring the Redcoats into the rough passes where they might be ambushed.

But Greene disapproved. His scouts brought in word that the hated Cornwallis was burning his train of baggage wagons. "This means," decided Nat Greene, "that the British will chase us wherever we go. Cornwallis is getting ready to travel light."

General Greene explained his plan, and it was smart and bold. He would retreat to the north, keeping just in front of the Redcoats—but not too close. Old Dan Morgan shook his head. He said this was not a good plan. He pointed out that on a retreat troops have a hard time keeping their spirits up. Morgan felt his commander was making a bad mistake.

But General Greene did not scare. He was anxious to lead Cornwallis deeper into the Carolina country where guerrillas could harass him day and night. So Greene gave the order to march north. Cornwallis followed in hot pursuit.

The British general knew there were many rivers in the

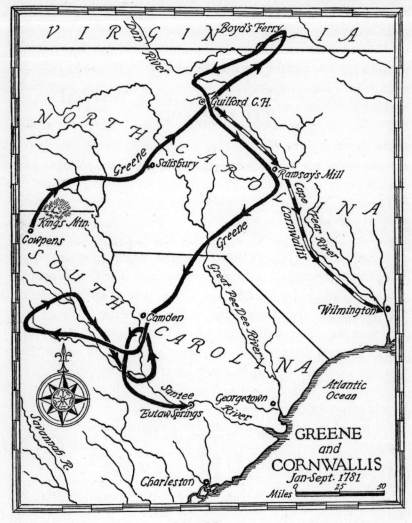

MAP No. 19

country ahead. He wanted to catch Nat Greene and his men with their backs to a river so they could not retreat, or to find half of the patriots on one side and half on the other. The rains turned roads to gumbo, and the British threw away equipment to lighten their loads. The ragged patriots were not troubled; they had nothing to throw away.

The campaign became a race for the rivers. Greene was in the saddle day and night. He went for a week without rest and without changing his clothes. Brigadier General Dan Morgan became worn out, and General Greene had to let him go home.

There was no rest for the Americans. Cornwallis was close behind, pushing his troops hard.

But the deeper into North Carolina they went, the happier General Greene became, for the British were getting farther and farther from their base in South Carolina. Now the *British* soldiers were hungry, and there was no food because the country was devastated. There were sharp patrol actions. In a retreat such as the Americans were making, one or two brave men left behind in good cover can delay the enemy for an hour. Cornwallis's men often had to spread out and go ahead slowly. At times they thought they had General Nat Greene trapped but they closed in only to find smoky campfires.

Finally, Lord Cornwallis reached the Dan River to discover the Americans were safely across in Virginia, and that they had tied up every available boat on the far bank.

Cornwallis was baffled. He faced a dilemma. He wanted to fight the enemy, but if he crossed the river he knew he would have to battle a reinforced army because patriots in Virginia were available to help Greene. The British needed food badly. There were no beef cattle along the riverbanks and no help could be expected from the citizens of North Carolina in the vicinity, for they resented the overbearing ways of the British. And last but

not least, Cornwallis was one hundred and forty miles from his nearest base, and supplies of all kinds were in demand.

Cornwallis solved the situation by withdrawing forty miles south of the Dan River and by making his men work to get food from the people of North Carolina. He made a bold announcement; he said the rebellion in North Carolina was over and that once again the colony was entirely under the rule of the King. But few believed him.

Raw, rainy weather hindered everyone, and both sides had many men on the sick list. But the Americans were fortunate in receiving valuable supplies. They were forwarded by a Danish patriot in Philadelphia, Christian Febiger ("Old Denmark"), a fine soldier who was heading the supply system in Philadelphia.

General Nat Greene was not a general to lie idle and wait for the breaks. He decided to attack the attackers even though his patriots suffered in the cold March weather because they were ill-clothed. It was the old story: half-starved Americans in rags and tatters, poorly shod, marching, marching, marching. General Greene displayed great courage and will power, and his men reflected his attitude. Finally, General Greene decided he was ready to fight on ground he himself had selected.

The place was Guilford Court House in North Carolina. Nat Greene was confident, for his troops outnumbered Cornwallis's. The count was small: four thousand five hundred Americans to one thousand nine hundred soldiers of the King—and the stakes were large.

The idea of fighting appealed to Cornwallis. For two months he had acted like a hound in pursuit of a fox and he was tired of the chase.

Greene decided to try the fighting plan the Old Wagoner had used at Cowpens: a "round-robin attack." But there was trouble. First, there was no river at the Americans' back. Secondly, the woods caused confusion. When certain units streaked for the rear according to plan, other American units became panicky. Men of the two sides became embroiled in fierce close-in fighting. Now Lord Cornwallis gave a horrible command. He ordered his cannoneers to fire grapeshot at the rebels, but the two sides were so close that the grapeshot cut down Redcoats and patriots alike. The hardhearted British general accomplished what he was after, for the cannonade was too much for Nat Greene's men and they retired, but many British soldiers died as a result of British grapeshot.

The battle was a Redcoat victory; however, Lord Cornwallis lost one fourth of his command. When news of the battle reached England, a leader in Parliament said, "Another such victory will ruin the British Army." Nevertheless, Cornwallis gave thanks to God for "complete victory."

On the next day, before he left the scene, Cornwallis tried to make his prisoners take the King's Oath. But while one of his officers was making a speech to tempt the captives to desert, the sound of the morning guns from Nat Greene's camp echoed in the hills. An old "Tar Heel" soldier, who had been taken prisoner, shouted defiantly, "Listen, boys! The old cock is crowing again."

The British headed for the seacoast. At Wilmington, South Carolina, they picked up needed supplies, then made a long march north to join the British forces which Sir Henry Clinton had dispatched to Virginia.

With his enemy gone, General Greene marched quickly into South Carolina and reduced British posts. He lost a battle at Camden and one at Eutaw Springs, but the British were forced to withdraw to their strongholds on the coast: Charleston and Savannah. General Greene summed up his campaign, "We fight, get beat, rise, and fight again."

General Nat Greene was forceful, tireless, farsighted and spirited—you could say he was a leader who would not stay beaten. His nine hundred-mile march was a campaign of heartbreak and suffering, but the result paved the way to the final American victory at Yorktown.

Trouble now returned to the old dominion state of Virginia. The traitor, Benedict Arnold (now a British brigadier), sailed out of New York Harbor for the James River on a raid. With the turncoat were one thousand six hundred men in twenty-seven British warships, all bent on destruction. While the raiders could not be expected to occupy the state, they were bent on doing as much damage as possible, for Virginia was one of the principal states supplying the Continental soldiers.

Von Steuben, the drillmaster, did his best to get militia in a position where it could fight Arnold, but he was not successful. Von Steuben, who was in Petersburg, Virginia, sent a small force to fight the traitor and his raiders. But Steuben's men were recruits and not powerful.

In the meantime, Arnold was in Richmond applying the torch to hundreds of buildings and to supplies—to everything but tobacco. That could be sold at a profit. Arnold was working his hardest at destruction. He was anxious to show the British they had made no mistake in engaging his services.

It seemed to Washington that he now had a chance to capture the traitor. A storm dispersed the British warships that were blockading the French men-of-war in Newport, so Washington asked the French please to send their ships south to trap Arnold. This was a popular move in the American headquarters. The patriots hated Arnold.

But the French sent only three warships to Virginia—not enough to do the job.

This French "effort" exasperated Washington. He lost his temper. He criticized the French, and this did not help the joint effort against the enemy. In reality, the French had not acted because Arnold's raid in Virginia seemed small to them.[1]

In Virginia, the British now came out with a form of barbarism which infuriated the horse-loving Virginians. Lord Cornwallis and his fierce dragoon chief, Ban Tarleton, up from the Carolinas, were doing everything possible to discourage the Virginians who were not loyal to the King. The British burned homes and looted on a large scale. To keep the patriots from using the fine-blooded horses, the Redcoats cut the throats of hundreds of horses and colts.

This war, like every war, was cruel. Everyone in America suffered to some degree. The families of the men who were in action often suffered real distress and want. But the people who suffered most, more even than the wounded, were the unfortunates who were captured.

---

[1] Later, Arnold was sent to raid New London, Connecticut, which he did ruthlessly enough. When he went to England, where he made his home, he was received by King George with open arms. But few Englishmen respected Benedict Arnold.

Chapter 26

PRISONERS OF WAR

BOTH sides treated prisoners horribly. Perhaps the British treated their captives worse than the patriots, because Lord George Germain, the King's minister, thought that the rebels were guilty of treason. He believed that when a rebel was captured the way in which he was handled did not matter, and that he was not entitled to humane care. Germain's idea set an evil course.

At first, the British sent many captives to England. But this was expensive, so they began to employ old ships as prisons. The worst prison hulk was the old ship, *Jersey*.

The *Jersey* lay anchored in a salt marsh called Wallabout Bay in the East River across from New York City. Prisoners aboard the hulk were seldom allowed to come on deck for air or sunshine. They were shut below decks, where it was dark and where only a breath of air could find its way through the few tiny ports. The unfortunates aboard the *Jersey* existed on a starvation diet of wormy bread, spoiled beef, and little water. No prisoner was allowed to bathe. Those who became sick were seldom removed to a hospital ship. The guards were horribly brutal and took pleasure in tormenting and torturing the captives. The *Jersey* was an unspeakably foul place. It was a terrible sight to see a fine-looking, healthy young man a few months after he had been brought aboard the *Jersey*. He was a broken wreck, covered with lice.

On the *Jersey* the guards started the day with the shout, "Rebels, turn out with your dead!" The prisoners fought to go ashore on burial details, where they dug shallow graves in the sand, because it was a chance to get off the ship for a short time. The hideous business of lying idle all day in the dark holds broke men. In summer the hulks were ovens; in winter, iceboxes. The unfortunates often tried to set fire to the hulk, for they felt they would just as soon burn as die a death of slow torture. The exact number of patriots who perished in Wallabout Bay is not known. It was probably several thousand.

But not every British prison ship was a disgrace. The hulk, *Good Hope*, commanded by Captain Charles Nelson and anchored in the North River, was a far better place than the *Jersey* because Captain Nelson took care of his prisoners.

The Americans used prison ships, too. They anchored them off New London and in Boston Harbor. The guards on these ships were often brutal, and the food just as bad as that aboard the average British floating prison.

At the Simsbury mines in Connecticut, the Americans mistreated British captives in the worst possible way. The prisoners were confined seventy feet below ground. They were crowded, bullied, and starved. The air in the mines was so stale that the prisoners burned charcoal in pots to try to suck in fresh air. The stench of the place was sickening.

When the American Army was suffering from lack of food and clothing, its prisoners suffered even more.

When prisoners escaped from British prisons early in the war, word spread rapidly about the treatment the captives were receiving. George Washington immediately became concerned.

He said that capturing prisoners was important, and that the more prisoners taken the better treatment captive patriots would receive. He called Lord Howe's attention to the foul treatment meted out to American prisoners. Washington tried in other ways to help, even to the extent of offering his personal fortune, but there was scant improvement in the life of a patriot unfortunate enough to be a prisoner.

It was a long time before there was a system for the exchanging of prisoners of war. A few generals, colonels, and lieutenant colonels were exchanged, and that was all for several years. At Kings Mountain, in South Carolina, the Americans had a chance to help the situation because they captured six hundred prisoners; but there was little organization after the battle, and the prisoners were poorly guarded, so many escaped.

In England, the Liberal party worked to better the plight of soldiers in English prisons. Benjamin Franklin, in Paris, was also greatly interested in the treatment of the captives in England. When he could, he sent a shilling sterling to each American in the foul Mill Prison in Plymouth, and in Forton, its sister prison at Portsmouth.

The thought that occupies prisoners is to escape. The fact that the patriot prisoners usually lived a life beneath that of beasts of burden made them exceedingly anxious to get away. But in Mill and Forton prisons, escapees who were recaptured were tortured by being placed in dark holes so small they had a hard time entering them. And at other times, recaptured men were impressed into the British Navy. There was little hope for a prisoner who escaped and who was unfortunate enough to be brought back.

When Ethan Allen was finally exchanged after serving three years as a prisoner, he published his experiences. His tale brought home to thousands the terrible life of a captive. Ethan wrote of how he had been placed aboard a British schooner of war, his hands and feet confined in leg irons, and how he lived on a wooden chest in the bottom of the ship. His leg irons weighed over thirty pounds. At night, in order to lie down on the chest, he inserted small blocks of wood in his shackles so there would be less pressure on his ankles.

Ethan gave all the gruesome details. He told of jailers spitting in his face, of being knocked down while he was handcuffed, of suffering for fresh water, of a diet in which a crust of bread was a banquet, of the sickening and perpetual stench, and of the darkness of the bottom of the ship. Ethan Allen had a strong body. He survived while others perished.

Prisoners who were finally exchanged and returned to their homes, broken in health and diseased, spurred other patriots into enlisting. Americans became angry at the treatment their soldiers received as prisoners. But the patriots themselves were not guiltless.

Chapter 27

THE AMERICAN NAVY

IT was not long after the fighting began before American sea-faring people captured thousands of "sea dogs" of Old England. The independent seamen on American privateers were gambling, for privateering was a dangerous game ending in either watery graves or high stakes, and when high stakes were gained prisoners were taken.

Although the Revolution was principally a land war, many colonists were at home on the sea. The hard-bitten privateersmen played a vital role in George Washington's idea of raiding British commerce. American seamen brought in important supplies, and before the war stopped they captured great numbers of British merchant ships.

The first sea fight gave an example of the determination that could be expected from the seafaring people of the colonies. In the tiny coastal town of Machias, Maine, there lived the O'Briens, a Yankee family of Irish descent. The eldest of the O'Briens was Jeremiah—an athlete who could wrestle. He could swing a woodman's ax for hours. When news of Lexington and Concord arrived in the village, Jeremiah, his brothers, and friends raised a Liberty Pole. This was a tall tree, stripped of all but its topmost branches and transplanted so it stood in the center of town. The patriots gathered about it and pledged themselves to freedom. Shortly the people of Machias were put to a test.

In June, 1775, two American sloops belonging to a Tory of the village sailed into the harbor with food. These ships, the *Unity* and the *Polly*, had been doing this for years—the idea was to exchange the food for lumber which the Tory could sell in Boston. Right on the sterns of the two ships was the British armed schooner, *Margaretta* (Midshipman Moore commanding). The *Margaretta*'s job was to protect the Tory, his two ships, his food, and the lumber.

When the Tory came ashore, Jeremiah O'Brien refused to have anything to do with the deal. He saw war ahead and he suspected that the British Army in Boston could use lumber.

Midshipman Moore took a look around the village and stopped before the Liberty Pole. "That must come down," Moore said, "or I'll order the *Margaretta* to fire on the town." While the patriots were considering the order, the *Margaretta*'s crew robbed a sloop belonging to an American, a Captain Toby, and took Captain Toby's provisions.

The O'Brien brothers and their friends held a secret town meeting. Shortly after this, with Jeremiah in the lead, they seized the Tory's ship, *Unity*, and prepared to sail down the harbor to fight. The father of the O'Briens told his sons good-by at the wharf.

When Midshipman Moore, on board the *Margaretta*, saw the *Unity* coming, he decided to sail away. But the O'Briens overhauled the *Margaretta*. When the two vessels were close, Midshipman Moore yelled, "Ship ahoy! Keep off, or I will fire!"

Jeremiah shouted, "In America's name, I demand your surrender!"

The *Margaretta* answered with a blast from her stern guns, killing one man. The Americans fired back with muskets. The

two vessels collided, and the Americans boarded the Britisher carrying pitchforks. The *Margaretta*'s crew fired their small arms, then charged with bayonets. The sea battle lasted one hour, ending at noon. Finally, above the bark of guns, someone on the *Margaretta* yelled, "I surrender! I surrender!"

The smoke on deck was blinding. "Who's that?" shouted Jeremiah. "If you surrender, throw down your arms."

The weapons of the *Margaretta*'s crew clattered to the deck. In a moment, Jeremiah cut down the British Union Jack. America had won her first sea fight.

Later, in another sea fight, Captain Jeremiah O'Brien was

captured and became one of the wretched souls locked up in Mill Prison. However, he escaped, was rowed to France, and returned to America.

In October, 1775, the Continental Congress saw that it would be a great advantage to have a navy, so it ordered that two ships of war be constructed. In September, two battalions of marines were formed. Then came an order for thirteen men-of-war. Esek Hopkins, a seaman from Rhode Island, a daring privateer raider of the French and Indian War, was made commander in chief of the navy with a salary of $125 a month.

Life aboard a man-of-war was hard. The ship's company was a human machine that obeyed the captain's orders on the jump. The seamen were divided into companies; some were trained to climb the rigging and handle the sails; others took care of the decks; the gunners were responsible that the cannon fired when ordered. At night the crew swung their hammocks (which served as beds) on the berth deck. Also on board were marines— sea soldiers, trained to climb high into the rigging in combat so they could fire down at the enemy's sailors. The marines were also ready to board other vessels, and fight close-in combat on a hostile deck. At night the marines were the sentinels.

Several times a day on a man-of-war, the captain had his drummers sound the "Beat to quarters." At this signal every man ran to his post. Powder and ball were brought to the guns, and the ship was prepared for action. The crew worked long, hard hours and the food was not very good. It was often salt pork, salt beef, or salt fish. Hard tack was the bread, and maybe twice a day the crew was served rum mixed with water, called "grog."

The discipline was more severe than in the army. It had to be, for a few minutes of sloppy work could cost the life of the crew and a ship. In the Revolution, the punishment with the "cat" was still in use. The victim was lashed to a framework and the cat-o'-nine tails was whipped against his bare back. This barbaric custom was so harsh that it often broke the spirits and some-times the health of the victims.

The colonies had few war vessels. The state navies had some and they were used to protect seacoast towns.[1] People realized that it would take a Continental Navy to stand up against the British Navy, and no American Navy was available.

The count in 1776 was one-sided. The Americans had three thousand seamen and twenty-seven ships. The British Navy had eighteen thousand sailors and one hundred twelve warships.[2]

The best thing the Americans had in the Revolution was courage. As far as sea fighting went, it seemed to them that a daring scheme was best—they would carry the war to enemy waters regardless of the size of the two navies.

The first American man-of-war to sail into enemy waters was the *Reprisal*. This ship carried Ben Franklin to France after raiding the West Indies. In 1777, more American ships preyed on British commerce. This was warfare unparalleled.

Late in 1777, into European seas sailed one of the most daring "sea wolves" of all time—John Paul Jones.

John Paul Jones first went aboard ship at the age of twelve. He was slender, of average height, and he had a temper. The speech of this American carried a trace of a burr from the coun-try of his birth—Scotland. In his early days on the ocean Jones had served in the African slave trade, but the cruelty of the business disgusted him and he quit it. Later, on a merchantman, he stopped a mutiny from spreading by striking a sailor with a belaying pin. He was tried and acquitted.

When war hit, John Paul Jones was the owner of a fine planta-tion in Virginia. Congress asked him for his views on war at sea. This was the actual beginning of the American Navy.

[1] The colonies of Massachusetts, Rhode Island, New York, Connecticut, Mary-land, Virginia, North and South Carolina had navies.

[2] At the end of the war, the British Navy numbered about one hundred thousand men; the Continental Navy never exceeded three thousand men.

But to the amazement of John Paul Jones, when Congress purchased ships, he found himself commissioned as a *lieutenant* instead of as a captain. But he did not quit, and soon (because his captain failed in a sea battle) John Paul Jones was made captain of an American war vessel.

In 1776, on the quarterdeck of the *Alfred*, John Paul Jones raised the first American naval flag which bore the motto, *"Don't Tread on Me."*

Later, John Paul Jones read a famous resolution from Congress proclaiming the first Stars and Stripes and, in the second paragraph, he saw his orders:

> RESOLVED, *That Captain John Paul Jones be appointed to Command the ship RANGER.*

Jones liked this. "The flag and I are twins," he said. The American flag has never had a braver man, or a harder fighter, raise it to the top of a mast.

Jones sailed the *Ranger* to France, where he looked up Ben Franklin. Dr. Franklin told him of a powerful man-of-war which was being built in Amsterdam—the *Indien*. She would carry a crew of four hundred and would have forty-six guns. "It would be a fine thing," mused Dr. Franklin, "if John Paul Jones could be given the *Indien* to fight in European waters."

But there was a mad scramble of international politics involving the ship. To learn about the fabulous ship, Franklin sent John Paul Jones in disguise to Amsterdam. Jones, a swarthy individual who spoke Spanish fluently, was made up to resemble a Spanish officer. He outwitted everyone on this trip and returned to France. He informed Dr. Franklin that the *Indien* was not ready, that it would be impossible to obtain her until the political picture changed. So Dr. Franklin told Jones to go to sea and carry out his orders to cruise the British coasts.

The *Ranger* sailed north. Jones was not afraid, although he was sailing into the lion's mouth—into British man-of-war territory.

Jones steered his ship through the narrow limits of the Irish Sea and stormed ashore at Whitehaven, Scotland. It looked as if Captain Jones and his crew were going to fight the Empire alone.

The idea of this intrepid fighter was to burn English shipping. But he had trouble. Half of his crew mutinied, partly from fear, partly because they did not wish to destroy ships they might take as prizes. Captain Jones had difficulty with his men, but he managed to spike British cannon at the harbor's entrance and this put the cannon out of commission. When news of his landing and his devilment spread, the London newspapers screamed for his capture.

Now Captain Jones sailed the *Ranger* across the Irish Sea to attack H.M.S. *Drake*. But the *Drake* sailed out of a harbor near Belfast on the lookout for Jones. The battle was fought within hailing distance and closer. Finally, the *Ranger* wrecked the *Drake*. The papers in England now demanded Jones's life.

The alarm in England was great. Insurance rates on cargoes and ships skyrocketed. The British referred to Jones as a privateer, a thief, and a pirate. They refused to regard him as what he was —a daring officer of the Continental Navy. Had they captured him, he probably would have been hanged. The British Admiralty was furious.

When Jones made port in France he found himself a hero, but the *Ranger* was taken from him and sent home. Captain Jones was promised another ship. He waited nine months. Finally, he was given an old Indian merchantman which was not a ship-of-war. It was a vessel in very bad condition.

Jones rechristened the ship the *Bonhomme Richard* in honor of his friend, Ben Franklin. To arm this ship, Jones traveled over much of France. But even with Ben Franklin's help, the best Jones could do was to secure old, condemned cannon. He also had a hard time getting a crew; and when he got one, only one fifth of its men could speak English. He had men from France, Switzerland, Portugal, Norway, America, Italy, Spain, India, England, Scotland, Ireland, Sweden, and several smaller countries. It took strict discipline and real leadership to command such a crew.

Finally, Captain Jones sailed the *Bonhomme* for Ireland. Following were four ships under his command. But Jones was unlucky. One of the ships, the *Alliance*, was commanded by Pierre Landais, an odd, unpredictable officer who had been thrown out of the French Navy. In addition to being peculiar, Landais was jealous of Captain Jones. And the *Alliance* had hardly cleared port when her crew mutinied. The voyage had an ill start.

The date of one of the hottest fights in naval history is September 23, 1779. On that day, lookouts for John Paul Jones sighted a British convoy of forty-one sail. The captains of two of Jones's ships did not want to attack. They were afraid. Jones sent for them and argued for hours. The two captains thought the odds too great.

Finally, John Paul Jones crowded on every possible sail and headed toward the convoy. The two captains who did not want to fight had little choice but to follow.

The enemy convoy scattered and headed for England. The convoy guards, *Scarborough* and *Serapis*, flying the Union Jack, sailed for the *Bonhomme Richard*. It was seven in the evening. Daylight was fading, but soon a full moon came up.

At the start of the fight, two of the worthless guns on the *Bonhomme Richard* burst, killing their gun crews. Then the weird Captain Landais would not help Jones! Landais stood off a mile and watched the powerful *Serapis* and the *Bonhomme* smash each other with broadsides.

Captain Jones ordered his cannon to fire at the mast of the *Serapis* so as to cut down the Britisher's ability to maneuver. The ships closed. Later Jones wrote, "The enemy's bowsprit came over the *Bonhomme*'s poop by the mizzenmast." Jones seized a cable and helped make the two ships fast. The cannon thundered. Holes were soon smashed clear through each ship. Fire broke out on the *Bonhomme* in two places. The marines swept the decks with musketry. The cries of the wounded were interspersed with the roars of the guns. The ships quivered from the beating they were taking.

The fifty guns of the *Serapis* threw 315 pounds of metal in a single broadside. The forty-two guns of Jones's ship fired only 258 pounds of metal when all of the guns on one side fired. The slaughter was horrible. Over seven hundred men were battling at night at close quarters to kill each other. Later, Henry Gardner, quarter-gunner of the *Bonhomme Richard*, wrote, "The whole deck was slippery with blood and littered with fragments of heads, bodies, and limbs."

The crazy Captain Landais sailed closer and ordered his gunners to fire into *both* ships! The men on the *Bonhomme* screamed at Captain Landais to stop, but this had no effect.

The *Bonhomme* started to sink. Jones had a crew fasten grappling hooks on the *Serapis*. If the hooks and cables held, maybe the *Bonhomme* would drag her enemy to the bottom.

The captain of the *Serapis* screamed, "Are you ready to surrender?"

"No," shouted Captain Jones, "I have just begun to fight!"

Boarders from the *Bonhomme* fought their way aboard the *Serapis* and came back.

It was reported that Captain John Paul Jones, who had twelve pistols in a belt around his waist and a cutlass in his hand, shot some of his men who deserted their posts. A daredevil on the *Bonhomme*, Midshipman Fanning, crawled out on a yardarm over the *Serapis* and dropped hand grenades through an open port. An explosion occurred on the British ship. John Paul Jones sprang for the *Serapis*. His men followed. Soon, Captain Pearson of the *Serapis* surrendered his sword to John Paul Jones.

The wounded were carried from the *Bonhomme* to the Britisher; the cables cut; and the *Bonhomme Richard* sank slowly, "peacefully," Jones wrote, "with her dead into about forty fathoms." Now Jones ordered the carpenters to rig temporary masts and to repair as much damage as possible so he could sail the *Serapis* to France and to safety.

The Britisher, *Countess of Scarborough*, surrendered to Jones's ship, *Pallas*.

The poet, Walt Whitman, in his "An Old-Time Sea Fight" tells of this bloody fight:

Would you hear of an old-time sea-fight?
Would you learn who won by the light of the moon and stars?

We closed with him, the yards entangled, the cannons touch'd
My captain lash'd fast with his own hands.

We had receiv'd some eighteen pound shots under water,
On our lower-gun-deck two large pieces had burst at the first fire,
    killing all around and blowing up overhead.

Fighting at sun-down, fighting at dark,
Ten o'clock at night, the full moon well up, our leaks on the gain,
    and five feet of water reported,
The master-at-arms loosing the prisoners confined in the afterhold
    to give them a chance for themselves.

The transit to and from the magazine is now stopt by the sentinels,
They see so many strange faces they do not know whom to trust.

Our frigate takes fire,
The other asks if we demand quarter?
If our colors are struck and the fighting done?

Now I laugh content, for I hear the voice of my little captain,
We have not struck, he composedly cries, *we have just begun our
  part of the fighting.*

Only three guns are in use,
One is directed by the captain himself against the enemy's main-mast,
Two well serv'd with grape and canister silence his musketry and
  clear his decks.

Not a moment's cease,
The leaks gain fast on the pumps, the fire eats toward the powder-
  magazine.

One of the pumps has been shot away, it is generally thought we are
  sinking.

Serene stands the little captain,
He is not hurried, his voice is neither high nor low,
His eyes give more light to us than our battle-lanterns

Toward twelve there in the beams of the moon they surrender to us.

John Barry, Continental naval officer from County Wexford,
Ireland, was also a great fighter. He commanded the brig, *Lexington,* in 1776, when she captured the British tender, *Edward*
—the first British vessel taken by a commissioned American ship.
Like Jones, Barry was a leader who was not dismayed when he
faced superior forces.

In spite of the efforts to raise funds by men like Robert Morris
and Ben Franklin, the Americans did not have an effective navy
in this war. The British Navy was far too powerful to be swept
aside.

Chapter 28
THE SURRENDER

CONTROL of most of the ocean gave the British a big advantage. The American Revolution seemed to be sputtering, and the crash in the American Army at the opening of the year 1781 added to that idea. The two mutinies had shaken the army.

In late January, George Washington climbed into a rowboat at the end of a wintry day after inspecting the fortress at West Point, New York. Light was fading from the gray sky, and Crow's Nest Mountain looked as bleak as the American cause itself.

The small crew of the rowboat shoved off from the snow-covered beach and began a six-mile row to take General Washington back to his headquarters at New Windsor. The river was clogged with ice; it was hard to see ahead. A biting north wind banged ice cakes against the boat. Waves began to wash over the sides. Washington, according to Count Dumas of the French Army, who was a passenger in the craft, said, "Courage, my friends! I will steer. My place is at the helm."

But even with a leader like General Washington at the helm of the patriots' cause, the Revolution looked as if it were failing. The soldiers were hungry and poorly clothed. Contractors, who had no principles, were raking in money and giving little in return. The treasury was almost empty. Relations with the French were ragged. There was graft in the hospitals containing American sick and wounded. The traitorous turncoat, Benedict Arnold, was looting Virginia, and this was particularly hard on Washington because he was unable to go and defend his home state. British affairs in Virginia seemed well fixed, for Cornwallis, up from the Carolinas, had seven thousand two hundred men, and the great Frenchman, General Lafayette, was beaten in a skirmish at Williamsburg.

Now, from New York, General Clinton of the British Army sent special orders to General Cornwallis in Virginia. These orders told Cornwallis to move his army either to the small tobacco port of Yorktown or to Williamsburg. Cornwallis chose Yorktown. Strange as it seems, this set the stage for the final act of the Revolution.

Far to the north of this tobacco harbor, at Newport, Rhode Island, was a French general who was anxious to fight the British. He was a real leader, a man not easily rattled, and who had presence of mind. The four thousand French soldiers under Lieutenant General Jean de Rochambeau were disciplined. Rochambeau was happy about his instructions from his king, Louis XVI, who had ordered that he place his men under Washington's command.

There was some doubt in Washington's mind as to when he could use this French force, but finally good fortune hit. General Rochambeau received word from the leader of the French fleet in the West Indies that his fleet was sailing in August for Chesapeake Bay. The admiral who sent the message was François de Grasse.

When George Washington heard of this, he saw that he could strike the British a blow. He ordered General Rochambeau to bring his soldiers to New York. Washington's idea was to make a secret march south and fight Cornwallis. He decided to leave enough men to protect West Point. He would combine with Rochambeau's men and attack Cornwallis from the land side while Admiral de Grasse struck from the sea.

It was a bold plan but it was dangerous. Washington was taking a chance, but he figured that in warfare every plan has an element of danger. He was worried. *Suppose*, he thought, *that the British leave their defenses about New York City, capture West Point, and attack us while we are on the march south?* This was a real cause for concern, for General Clinton in New York City had enough troops to do this. But General Washington refused to be stopped by his fears. The secret march to Virginia began. Only the highest officers knew where Washington was leading his men. In this way, spies and deserters were unable to tell the British.

There was trouble among the American troops. It had been a long time since they were paid; they needed money to send to their loved ones; and these soldiers, many of whom were from New England, New York, Pennsylvania, and New Jersey, were not pleased about heading south away from their homes.

Robert Morris helped the situation. As superintendent of finance, he borrowed twenty thousand dollars from the generous General Rochambeau. The French King also sent money. This, and General Washington's enthusiasm to win, as well as his iron will, kept the troops on the road.

Philadelphia welcomed the two armies as they trudged through the dusty city. Congress reviewed the troops. The members removed their hats when Washington and Rochambeau rode by. Bands played. The French Army had the best-uniformed troops in the world and they impressed Congress and the Philadelphians.

There was a banquet for the principal patriots. In the midst

MAP NO. 20

of the toasting, a courier arrived with a message for the French minister. The diplomat stood up from his place at the table and gave exciting news—"Thirty-six ships of the line, with French soldiers aboard, commanded by Admiral de Grasse, are in Chesapeake Bay. His soldiers are already in touch with the Marquis de Lafayette in Virginia."

There was an uproar of happiness. Washington's plan hinged

on the arrival of the French fleet. It was now in position to guard the entrance of Chesapeake Bay.

About ten days after the big French fleet arrived at the mouth of the Chesapeake, British warships appeared. Broadsides were exchanged. In the battle, the French had more sailors killed than the enemy, but a number of British warships were badly damaged and withdrew. This Battle of the Chesapeake was not a sea fight famous for exciting action, but because the British fleet sailed afterward for New York to get repairs, this battle became one of the most important in history. Washington and Rochambeau could now take their men down the bay. Cornwallis was blocked from receiving help by sea.

The American and French armies marched on through Baltimore and were impressed by the straight streets and the sidewalks of the town.

Although General Washington had written ahead, there was shipping available at the head of the bay for only one thousand French troops and one thousand Americans. The rest continued to march. Some got rides down the bay at other points. The two armies assembled near Williamsburg.

The naval and land forces were now united to strike Cornwallis at Yorktown. Considering the lack of communication, an amazing effort involving long distances had been closely coordinated. The stage was set for final victory. For this brilliant work, the French leaders and General Washington must be given credit.

Cornwallis realized his danger. He was on a peninsula. His scouts reported that many barges and sailing vessels packed with enemy had gone up the James River, on the far side of the Peninsula. It was obvious that he and his six thousand men would soon be attacked. They welcomed a battle, but they were on a bad piece of ground for a last-ditch fight. The Britisher had over two thousand men sick. Tories from Portsmouth flocked to him for protection. This meant more mouths to feed.

General Cornwallis sent word to General Clinton in New York City of his plight. Cornwallis wanted Clinton to bring warships, troops, and supplies. But Clinton could not make up his mind to leave New York. He had his own worries.

Cornwallis decided to build a large fort occupying about a square half-mile. He found that he was short of tools. Nevertheless, he and his men managed to construct a formidable fortress around Yorktown, guarded by three smaller forts called redoubts.

On a fine day in the early fall, Washington gave the word to start his army marching through the wooded Virginia countryside from Williamsburg to Yorktown. He was reinforced by Virginia militia and men from the French fleet. He had about seventeen thousand men ready to fight.

Washington planned siege warfare, and had Frenchmen with him who were masters at that. Von Steuben also was experienced in this type of fighting.

The American artillery went into position. Soon cannon balls banged into the British works. Zigzag trenches were dug by the attackers so as to get the musketmen closer to the British earthworks.

Cornwallis was in a deathtrap. He tried to escape by transporting his men across the river to Gloucester Point, where the American lines were lightly held, but a storm upset his plans.

The allies dug approach trenches closer and closer to the fort. Two of the redoubts were captured.

The cannons of the allies fired around the clock. The British and Germans took a beating. The walls of the fort began to crumble. Fire pouring into it became so heavy Cornwallis's cannoneers could not man their guns. Having little fire on them was a great advantage to the allied infantry. Cornwallis tried raids on his enemies but without success.

The sea routes were blocked. The biggest battleship in the world, *Ville de Paris*, was close at hand. The combined enemy forces were too strong for Cornwallis. There was still no sign of General Clinton.

On the morning of October 17, 1781, a British drummer braved the fire on the breastworks and beat a long roll. The allies recognized this as a signal that Cornwallis wanted a parley and they ceased fire. A British officer, well blindfolded, was led to General Washington's headquarters to arrange for surrender terms. The three weeks of siege were over. The year that had begun so disastrously for the Americans now looked wonderful.

The British officer who had been sent to George Washington

as a messenger said that General Cornwallis wanted a twenty-four-hour truce. Washington decided this was too much. He gave Cornwallis two hours to send his proposal in writing. Cornwallis agreed, and later signed the surrender proposal.

The formal surrender of the British was like a pageant, and an impressive one. The British and Germans looked gaudy in their uniforms as they marched out of the fort. The Americans demanded that the British bring their colors out cased, as General Lincoln had been forced to do at the surrender of Charleston. The British band played the tune, "The World Turned Upside Down." And it looked upside down. The Continental soldiers looked like scarecrows and the Virginia militia was almost as ragged.

Facing the Americans were the French in their full-dress uniforms of several colors. On their horses, out in front of their armies, were Generals Washington and Rochambeau and their staff officers.

The defeated army marched down the long avenue between the French and Americans and threw down its arms. General O'Hara, Cornwallis's second in command, led the way on his horse. Cornwallis was not in sight. He was inside the fort. He said he was sick.

General O'Hara rode up to General Rochambeau; apparently he was going to surrender to the French general. But Rochambeau indicated that Washington was in command. General O'Hara rode saddle-to-saddle alongside General Washington and gave the leader Cornwallis's sword. Washington had him give his sword to Lincoln—one second-in-command to another. The Revolution, which began with the Boston Massacre on March 5, 1770, was at an end. The date was October 19, 1781.

When Parliament heard of the surrender, it decided England was beaten. Parliament told the King to make peace. The colonies were free and could now form their own government. A new political era had begun.

No one knows the exact number of people who were killed in this war or how much property was destroyed. The number of killed and wounded has been dwarfed by later wars when greater numbers were involved. But the sacrifices of the Revolutionists and their allies gave birth to the greatest nation yet to appear on the face of the earth.

There are many reasons why the Americans and French won. One of these was that the British were fighting three thousand miles from home. Another was that the patriots received invaluable aid from France in the form of money, warships, cannon, ammunition, and other supplies. Foreign volunteers such as Lafayette, Von Steuben, Kosciusko, and others appeared at a critical time and gave their best.

The Continental riflemen and their best friends, the artillerymen, established military traditions under terrible conditions. They were able to do this because they were led by dedicated military leaders like Nat Greene, Henry Knox, Dan Morgan, Anthony Wayne—and Benedict Arnold until he performed his traitorous act. Lesser leaders supported the commander in chief with similar and splendid devotion.

The era produced many great Americans. Many of these worked for the Revolution far from the enemy. Benjamin Franklin, Robert Morris, Patrick Henry, and others helped beyond estimation. In the homes of the patriots, families suffered and made sacrifices so that the cause could succeed.

After the fighting stopped, there were problems to be solved. An American Peace Commission in Paris (Ben Franklin, John Jay, John Adams, and Henry Laurens) struggled to remove difficulty after difficulty, and not the least of these was to get England to recognize the colonies as *The United States of America*.

The war was won, but the country was far from united. The Tories were utterly crushed by England's defeat. Many, many Tories were fine people—some, descendants of the *Mayflower* pilgrims. Two great Americans, Alexander Hamilton and Patrick Henry, now took the lead in helping the Tories gain a peaceful life as American citizens. However, numbers of Tories refused to stay in the United States, where the feeling was strong against them. They moved to Canada.

The patriots won their independence, and as time went by people realized more and more the part played by George Washington. Washington was an intensely human man, a selfless person. He sometimes lost his temper. He understood men and he inspired them. Washington felt terrible when he saw his men suffering, marching barefooted in the snow, with "starvation rations" in the wagon train. But he did not feel so bad that his resolution to win was affected in the slightest degree. These are the facts of his character. Without George Washington, the Revolution would have collapsed.

Abraham Lincoln, one of the greatest Americans of all time, said, "Washington is the mightiest name on earth—long mightiest in the cause of civil liberty.... To add to the brightness of the sun, or glory to the name of Washington, alike is impossible. Let none attempt it. In solemn awe pronounce the name, and in naked deathless splendor leave it shining on."

AUTHOR'S NOTE

The ladies of the library staff, United States Military Academy, West Point, New York, headed by Miss Thelma Bedell, helped me to tell THE STORY OF THE REVOLUTIONARY WAR, for they located much of the material for this book. They were patient and interested. I thank them.

Lieutenant Colonel John R. Elting, Department of Military Art and Engineering at West Point, studied the manuscript, corrected it, and advised me.

My editor in chief at home, my wife, Dort Darrah Reeder, gave me invaluable help in many ways, and not the least of these was encouragement. And I also acknowledge with thanks the work of my typist, Mrs. Marion Humphrey.

RED REEDER

West Point, New York

240

FOR FURTHER READING

In writing this story, I referred to numerous volumes, some of them very old. My principal guideposts were:

American Military History, 1607-1953, Department of the Army, 1956.

The War of the Revolution (in two volumes), by Christopher Ward. New York: The Macmillan Company, 1952.

The American War of Independence in Perspective, by Lieutenant General Sir George F. MacMunn. London: G. Bell and Sons, 1939— a valuable book for the English point of view.

I benefited by the use of maps in the *Atlas*, edited by Colonel Vincent J. Esposito, Professor of Military Art and Engineering, United States Military Academy, West Point, New York. With his permission, some of the maps in this book are based upon maps in his *Atlas*.

SELECTED BOOKS

ABBOTT, JOHN S. C. *Paul Jones*. New York: Dodd & Mead, 1874.

ALDEN, JOHN RICHARD. *General Charles Lee*. Baton Rouge: Louisiana State University Press, 1951.

———. *The American Revolution*. New York: Harper & Brothers, 1954.

ARMBRUSTER, EUGENE L. *The Wallabout Prison Ships*. New York: 1920.

BAILEY, REV. J. D. *Some Heroes of the American Revolution*. Spartanburg, South Carolina: Band and White, 1924.

BOYNTON, CAPTAIN EDWARD C. *History of West Point*. New York: D. Van Nostrand, 1863.

BUELL, AUGUSTUS C. *Paul Jones*. Vols. I and II. New York: Dodd and Mead, 1905.

CARMER, CARL. *The Hudson*. New York: Farrar and Rinehart, 1939.

CLARKE, T. WOOD. *The Bloody Mohawk*. New York: The Macmillan Company, 1940.

CODMAN, JOHN, 2nd. *Arnold's Expedition to Quebec*. New York: The Macmillan Company, 1901.

DAVES, EDWARD G. *Maryland and North Carolina in the Campaign of 1780-1781*. Baltimore: 1893.

DORSON, RICHARD M. *America Rebels*. New York: Pantheon Books, Inc., 1953.

DUDLEY, E. LAWRENCE. *Benjamin Franklin*. New York: The Macmillan Company, 1915.

ECKENRODE, HAMILTON J. *The Story of the Campaign and Siege of Yorktown*. Washington, D.C.: United States Government Printing Office, 1931.

FRANKLIN, BENJAMIN. *Autobiography*. London: The Chesterfield Society, (undated).

FREEMAN, DOUGLAS SOUTHALL. *George Washington*. Vols. 3, 4, 5. New York: Charles Scribner's Sons, 1952.

GANOE, WILLIAM ADDLEMAN. *The History of the United States Army*. New York: D. Appleton-Century Co., 1942.

GUIZOT, M. *Washington*. New York: Jane Miller, 1863.

HALSEY, FRANCIS WHITING. *The Old New York Frontier*. New York: Charles Scribner's Sons, 1901.

HARTLEY, CECIL B. *The Life of Gen. Francis Marion*. Philadelphia: Davis, Porter and Coates, 1866.

HAVIGHURST, WALTER. *George Rogers Clark*. New York: McGraw-Hill Book Company, 1952.

HISLOP, CODMAN. *The Mohawk*. New York: Rinehart & Co., 1948.

HOUGH, FRANKLIN B. (editor). *Siege of Savannah*. Albany: J. Munsell, 1866.

HUGHES, RUPERT. *George Washington*. Vols. I and II. New York: William Morrow & Co., 1927.

JAMES, JAMES ALTON. *George Rogers Clark Papers, 1771-1781*. Virginia Series, Vol. III. Springfield, Illinois: Illinois State Historical Society, 1912.

JAMES, JAMES ALTON. *Kings Mountain*. National Park Service Historical Handbook Series #22. Washington, D.C.: 1955.

LANCASTER, BRUCE. *From Lexington to Liberty*. New York: Doubleday & Co., 1955.

LAWRENCE, ALEXANDER A. *Storm Over Savannah*. Athens, Georgia: University of Georgia Press, 1951.

LAWSON, ELIZABETH. *Samuel Adams*. New York: International Publishers, 1946.

LOSSING, B. F. *Pictorial Field Book of the Revolution*. Vols. I and II. New York: Harper Brothers, 1852.

MACLAY, EDGAR STANTON. *A History of the United States Navy*. Vol. I. New York: D. Appleton & Co., 1894.

MC CRADY, EDWARD. *The History of South Carolina in the Revolution—1775 to 1780*. New York: The Macmillan Company, 1901.

MONTROSS, LYNN. *Rag, Tag and Bobtail*. New York: Harper & Brothers, 1952.

MOORE, HUGH. *Memoir of Col. Ethan Allen*. Plattsburgh: O. R. Cook, 1834.

———. *Morristown*. National Park Service Historical Handbook Series #7. Washington, D.C.: 1950.

NORTON, A. TIFFANY. *History of Sullivan's Campaign*. Lima, New York: A. Tiffany Norton, 1879.

O'BRIEN, MICHAEL J. *An Irish Heroine of the War of the Revolution*. New York: The Journal of the American Irish Historical Society, 1916.

PELL, JOHN. *Ethan Allen*. New York: Houghton Mifflin Co., 1929.

PRATT, FLETCHER. *A Compact History of the United States Navy*. New York: Hawthorne Books, 1956.

RAVENEL, MRS. ST. JULIEN. *Charleston*. New York: The Macmillan Company, 1912.

RIEDESEL, FRIEDERIKA. *Letters and Journals Relating to the War of the American Revolution*. Albany: Joel Munsell, 1867.

ROBSON, ERIC. *Letters From America—1773 to 1780*. New York: Barnes and Noble, 1951.

ROSEWATER, VICTOR. *The Liberty Bell*. New York: D. Appleton and Co., 1926.

———. *Saratoga*. National Park Service Historical Handbook Series #4. Washington, D.C.: 1955.

SHERMAN, REV. ANDREW M. *Life of Captain Jeremiah O'Brien.* Morristown, New Jersey: Geo. W. Sherman, 1902.

SHERWIN, OSCAR. *Benedict Arnold.* New York: The Century Co., 1931.

SMITH, JUSTIN H. *Our Struggle for the Fourteenth Colony.* 2 vols. New York: G. P. Putnam Sons, 1907.

SONS OF THE AMERICAN REVOLUTION. *Early Sea Fights of the American Revolution.* Boston: New Bedford Chapter, 1928.

STODDARD, R.H. and SCUDDER, H. E. (editors). *Men and Manners in America One Hundred Years Ago.* New York: Scribner, Armstrong & Co., 1876.

―――. *Stony Point Battlefield.* New York: The American Scenic and Historic Preservation Society, 1902.

SULLIVAN, EDWARD DEAN. *Benedict Arnold, Military Racketeer.* New York: The Vanguard Press, 1932.

TAYLOR. *Martyrs to the Revolution.* (no nomenclature―undated).

―――. *The Journal of Isaac Senter.* Philadelphia: The Historical Society of Pennsylvania, 1846.

THOMAS, HENRY, and THOMAS, DANA LEE. *Living Biographies of Famous Americans.* Garden City, New York: Blue Ribbon Books, 1946.

THRUSTON, R. C. BALLARD. *The Origin and Evolution of the United States Flag.* H. Doc. No. 258, 69th Congress, 1st Session. Washington, D.C.: United States Government Printing Office.

VAN TYNE, CLAUDE H. *The Loyalists of the American Revolution.* New York: The Macmillan Company, 1902.

VAN DOREN, CARL. *Benjamin Franklin.* New York: The Viking Press, 1938.

―――. *Mutiny in January.* New York: The Viking Press, 1943.

WALLACE, WILLARD M. *Appeal to Arms.* New York: Harper & Brothers, 1951.

WHITE, KATHERINE K. *The King's Mountain Men.* Dayton, Virginia: Joseph K. Ruebush Co., 1924.

WIRT, WILLIAM. *Patrick Henry.* Philadelphia: James Webster, 1818.

WOODWARD, WILLIAM E. *Tom Paine.* New York: E. P. Dutton & Co., 1945.

―――. *Yorktown.* National Park Service Historical Handbook Series #14. Washington, D.C.: 1950.

INDEX

Abercromby, Gen., 45
Abney, "Long Sam," 202-06
Adams, John, 19, 45-57, 66, 238
Adams, Sam, 3-8, 12, 17, 18, 23, 37, 47
Albany, N. Y., 34, 107-13, 117
Allen, Ethan, 25-35, 56, 58, 116, 148-49, 217
Allen, Levi, 26-27
André, John, 164-69
Arnold, Benedict, 27-35, 55-64, 89, 101-02, 113, 116, 119-23, 160-69, 212-13, 231, 238
Attucks, Crispus, 21

Barry, John, 229
Beaumarchais, Pierre, 98, 115, 132
Bemis Heights, 118
Bennington, Vt., 116-17, 125
Bonhomme Richard, The, 226-29
Boston, Mass., 3-8, 17-23, 32, 36-37, 42, 47-48, 51, 53, 55, 58, 100
Boston "Massacre," 20-22
"Bounty jumpers," 194
Bounty system, 50, 194
Braddock, Gen., 10-11, 49, 205
Brandywine Creek, 126, 131
Brant, Joseph, 171, 175, 177
Breed's Hill, 37-43
Briand, Bishop, 57
"Brown Bess" musket, 4, 93
Brown, John, 56, 102

Bunker Hill, 36-43, 47, 77, 116
Burgoyne, John, 36-37, 103-04, 106-23, 131, 191, 206
Butler, John, 170, 175
Butler, Zebulon, 170-71

Cambridge, Mass., 40, 48
Camden, battle of, 191, 195, 199, 200, 204
Campbell, Lord William, 70
Campbell, William, 201-06
Canada, 28-29, 34-35, 55-64, 103-04, 116
Carleton, Sir Guy, 34, 56, 61, 88-90
Charleston, S. C., 37-43, 69-75, 77, 125, 185-89, 202
Charlotte, N. C., 204-06
Cherokee Indians, 75
Cherry Valley, N. Y., 172
Cheyney, Thomas, 126-27
Clark, George Rogers, 179-81
Cleveland, Ben, 202-06
Clinton, Henry, 36-37, 65, 70-75, 81, 120, 138, 140, 154-55, 159, 162, 164-65, 169, 182, 185-87, 197, 203, 206, 232, 235-36
Clowney, Sam, 199
Committees of Correspondence, 22
Committee of Public Safety, 27
Concord, Mass., 3-8, 25, 27, 30, 45, 67, 77
Connecticut, 23, 27, 40, 42, 76, 154-55, 157, 175, 213, 215, 223

245

Continental Army, 48
Continental Congress, 30-31, 44, 66-
    69, 106, 117, 131, 135, 138, 145,
    152-53, 163, 194-95, 198, 204, 222-
    23, 232
Conway Cabal, 137
Conway, Thomas, 137
Corbin, Molly, 86, 143
Cornwallis, Gen., 81, 96, 128, 188-89,
    191-92, 203-13, 231-39
Cowpens, 199-206, 211
Custis, Martha, 46

Dawes, William, 3-8
Deane, Silas, 103
Declaration of Independence, 65-68,
    78, 82, 98
Declaration of Rights, 18
de Grasse, François, 231-39
De Kalb, Gen., 191
Delaplane, William, 30
Delaware, 204
Delaware Indians, 181
Delaware River, 88, 90, 94-97, 131
de Rochambeau, Jean, 231-39
D'Estaing, Count, 149-52, 174, 184
Detroit, NWT, 179
Dickinson, John, 18, 67
Dinwiddie, Gov., 46
Dorchester Heights, Mass., 53
Dunmore, Earl of, 51, 65

East India Tea Company, 22-23
Enos, Roger, 63

Falmouth, Maine, 51, 65
Faneuil Hall, 20
Febiger, Christian, 210
Ferguson, Patrick, 200-03
Fort Anne, 109, 115
Fort Duquesne, 10
Fort Edward, 39, 109, 115
Fort Lee, 84-86, 143
Fort Stanwix, 111-13
Fort Ticonderoga, 28-35, 45, 52-53,
    59, 89, 103-04, 108-09, 115, 117,
    162
Fort Washington, 84-85

France, 92-93, 98, 102-03, 135, 138, 141,
    149-51, 174, 191, 195, 213, 222-23,
    225, 231-39
Franklin, Benjamin, 2-23, 32, 33, 97,
    98, 103, 133, 153, 172-74, 217, 224-
    39, 238
    Poor Richard's Almanac, 9, 12
    quoted in London Chronicle, 11
    to France, 92-93, 223
Freeman's Farm, 118-20
French and Indian War, 9, 23, 27, 45-
    46, 222
French Fleet, 138-39, 145-52, 183-84,
    195, 213, 231-39

Gadsden, Christopher, 18, 69
Gage, Thomas, 3-8, 22, 36, 37
Gansevoort, Peter, 111
Gaspee, H.M.S., 22
Gates, Horatio, 88, 117-23, 131, 174,
    190-91, 195, 204
George III, 5, 11, 13-23, 37, 42, 65, 67,
    79, 104, 134, 182, 186, 213, 237
Georgia, 11, 23, 42, 182
Germain, Lord George, 103, 106, 138,
    182, 185, 214
German Flats, N. Y., 171
German soldiers, 65, 80-81, 93-97, 107-
    23, 134-37, 182, 191, 235
Germantown, battle of, 129-32
Girty, Simon, 181
Green Mountain Boys, 25-35
Greene, Nathanael, 81, 127-28, 130,
    194-95, 203-13, 238
Grenville, George, 15

Hale, Nathan, 83-84
Halifax, Canada, 55
Hamilton, Alexander, 141-44, 239
Hamilton, "The Hair Buyer," 177-81
Hancock, John, 3-8, 18, 19, 32, 37,
    44, 145
Harlem Heights, 84
Harvard University, 7, 19
Henry, Patrick, 11, 15, 17-18, 23-25,
    66, 179, 181, 238-39
Herkimer, Nicholas, 111-13
Honeywell, John, 93
Hopkins, Esek, 222-23

Howe, "Black Dick," 78, 80, 82, 86, 131, 149
Howe, Robert, 182
Howe, William, 36, 40-42, 55, 76-90, 99, 104, 106, 124-38, 215
Hudson River, 56, 86, 100, 155
Hutchinson, Thomas, 17

Iroquois Indians, 104, 110-13, 171

Jasper, Sgt., 69-75, 184
Jay, John, 82, 238
Jefferson, Thomas, 32, 66
Jersey, prison ship, 214-18
Johnson, Guy, 110
Johnson, Thomas, 45
Jones, John Paul, 223-29

Kentucky, 177, 179
Kings Mountain, 199-206, 217
Kips Bay, 82, 84
Knowlton, Thomas, 84
Knox, Henry, 52-53, 103, 194, 196, 204, 238
Kosciusko, Thaddeus, 118-19, 163, 238

Lafayette, Marquis de, 98, 141-44, 195, 231-39
Lake Champlain, 28-35, 56, 88, 107-13
Lake George, 28, 33, 56, 107-13
Lamb, John, 18
Lancaster, Penna., 129
Langdon, John, 116
Laurens, Henry, 238
Laurens, John, 144
Lee, Charles, 45-47, 66, 70-75, 87-88, 91, 139-44
Lee, Henry (Light Horse Harry), 159-60, 169, 204-06
Lexington, Mass., 3-8, 25, 27, 30, 45, 67
Liberty Bell, 67
Liberty, The, 19-20, 40
Lincoln, Ben., 183-84, 187, 237
Logan Brothers, 202-06
Long Island, battle of, 76-83

MacDougall, Alex, 12
Magaw, Robert, 86

Maine, 51, 58, 60-63, 65, 219
Manchester, Vt., 115
Marion, Francis, 189-90, 204-06
Maryland, 11, 45, 67, 84, 123, 157, 204, 223
Massachusetts, 3-11, 23, 27, 50, 75, 116-17, 157, 223
McCrea, Jane, 114
Minutemen, 3-8
Mohawk Indians, 22, 45, 104, 110-13
Mohawk Valley, 110-18, 171-77
Monmouth, battle of, 140-44
Montcalm, Gen., 36, 39
Montgomery, Richard, 58-64
Montreal, 57, 59, 178
Montrose, Lord Marquess, 141
Morgan, Dan, 49, 61, 119-23, 141-44, 195, 204-09, 238
Morris, Gouverneur, 152
Morris, Robert, 98, 160, 229, 232, 238
Morristown, N. J., 97-99, 194
Moulton's Hill, 36-43
Moultrie, William, 71-75
Mount Vernon, Va., 17
Mowat, Henry, 51
Mutiny, 196-98

Navy, American, 219-29
Nelson, Charles, 215
New Hampshire, 93, 116, 149
New Haven, Conn., 193
New Jersey, 11, 76-90, 106, 125-26, 143, 144, 159-60, 194-95, 198, 232
Newtown, N. Y., battle of, 176
New York, 23, 25-35, 37, 42, 51, 75-90, 106, 120, 140, 149, 154, 161-69, 223, 232
New York City, 76-90, 203, 214
Norfolk, Va., 51
North, Lord, 22
North Carolina, 157, 187-88, 191-92, 199, 200-03, 207-13, 223, 231
Norwalk, Conn., 193
Northwest Territory, 177
"Not worth a Continental," 193

O'Brien, Jeremiah, 219-21
Oswego, N. Y., 104
Otis, James, 19-20

Paine, Tom, 65-66, 91-92
Parker, Jonas, 6-8
Parker, Sir Peter, 73-75
Paulding, John, 166
Paulus Hook, N. J., 159-60
Pennsylvania, 11, 23, 42, 62, 67, 84, 106, 123, 126, 154, 157, 170, 175, 196, 232
Philadelphia, 30-35, 47, 67, 93, 106, 118, 129, 131, 135, 137-38, 154, 160-69, 196, 232
Pickens, Andrew, 188
Pitcairn, British major, 6
Pitcher, Molly, 143
Pitt, William, 19, 133
Plains of Abraham, 36
Pontiac, Ottawa chief, 11
Princeton, N. J., 97, 116, 196
Privateers, 145-52, 222
Pulaski, Count, 184
Punishment, 50-51, 195, 214-18, 222-23
Putnam, Israel, 23, 39-43, 51, 81-90, 100

Quebec, 36, 57, 59-64, 89, 162
Quincy, Josiah, 12

Randolph, Peyton, 31
Ranger, The, 224-25
Reed, Joseph, 198
Revere, Paul, 3-8, 18
Rhode Island, 22-23, 50, 75, 148-49, 174, 184, 195, 204, 222-23, 231
Richmond, Va., 213
Riedesel, Baron, 107-13, 118-23
Rogers, Robert, 39, 116, 155
Romney, H.M.S., 20
Rutledge, John, 70-75, 186

Saratoga, 114-23, 131-39, 162
Savannah, Ga., 182-92
Schoharie County, N. Y., 132
Schuyler, Philip, 113, 117-23
Senter, Dr., 62-63
Serapis, The, 226-29
Seven Years' War, 5, 12, 132
Sevier, "Nolichucky Jack," 201-06
Shawnee Indians, 181
Shelby, Isaac, 201-06

Simcoe, Col., 154-55
Simsbury mines, Conn., 215
Smith, Francis, 6-8
Sons of Liberty, 18-20
South Carolina, 17, 23, 42, 65, 69-75, 184-92, 199-202, 204, 207-13, 217, 223, 231
Spain, 183
Stamp Act, 15, 18-19, 69
Stark, John, 93, 116
Stars and Stripes, first, 111
Staten Island, 79
St. Clair, Gen., 109, 117
St. Johns, Canada, 34, 58-59, 89, 109
St. Leger, Barry, 110-13, 118
Stony Point, battle of, 155-59
"Stormont," 93
Sullivan, John, 88, 149-52, 174-77
Sullivans Island, battle of, 70-75
Sumter, Thomas, 188

Talbot, Silas, 147-48
Tappan, N. Y., 168
Tarleton, Banastre, 186-89, 202, 204-06, 213
Taxes, 3, 12, 17, 19-23
Tea, 15-23, 32, 153
Tennessee, 200
Ticonderoga, see Fort Ticonderoga
Tories, 13, 18, 30-31, 37, 42, 53, 55, 69-70, 75-76, 90, 97, 104, 107-15, 132-33, 137, 154-55, 159-60, 170, 176-77, 183, 186-87, 192, 194, 200-03, 239
Townshend, Chas., 19
Trenton, N. J., 88, 94-97, 116, 131
Tryon, Gov., 26, 76, 77, 155

Valley Forge, 129, 131-39, 194
VanWart, Isaac, 166
Vermont, 25-35, 115-16, 149
Vincennes, 180-81
Virginia, 11, 23, 31, 46, 51, 84, 117, 123, 154, 157, 177, 181, 193, 200, 204, 209, 212-13, 223, 231-39
Virginia House of Burgesses, 15
von Steuben, Gen., 135-38, 140, 212, 238

Wallabout Bay, 214-18
Ward, Artemas, 40, 117

Warner, Seth, 34
Warren, Dr. Joseph, 3, 18, 20, 41-42
Washington, George, 17, 31, 44-57, 63, 70, 91-92, 97, 100-06, 117, 131-39, 174, 182, 194-98, 213, 215, 219
    and French fleet, 145-52
    at Morristown, 97-99
    at Stony Point, 155-59
    attack on Trenton, 93-96
    background, 46
    description, 46
    fighting—N. Y., N. J., 76-90
    final campaign, 230-39
    near Philadelphia, 124-30
    nominated as C.I.C., 47
    relationship with Arnold, 160-69

Valley Forge; results of Saratoga, 131-38
Waters, Daniel, 147
Wayne, Anthony, 128-30, 140, 156-59, 196-98, 238
West Point, N. Y., 100, 167, 196, 230, 232
    The Great Chain, 163-64
West Virginia, 200
Whigs, 13
White Plains, N. Y., 84
Williams, David, 166
Wyoming Valley, 170, 175

Yale University, 83
Yorktown, Va., 231-39